Reading STREET

## Program Authors

Peter Afflerbach
Camille Blachowicz
Candy Dawson Boyd
Wendy Cheyney
Connie Juel
Edward Kame'enui
Donald Leu

Jeanne Paratore
P. David Pearson
Sam Sebesta
Deborah Simmons
Sharon Vaughn
Susan Watts-Taffe
Karen Kring Wixson

**PEARSON**
Scott Foresman

**Editorial Offices:** Glenview, Illinois • Parsippany, New Jersey • New York, New York
**Sales Offices:** Boston, Massachusetts • Duluth, Georgia • Glenview, Illinois
Coppell, Texas • Sacramento, California • Mesa, Arizona

*We dedicate Reading Street to*
*Peter Jovanovich.*

*His wisdom, courage,*
*and passion for education*
*are an inspiration to us all.*

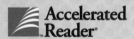

**About the Cover Artist**

Mark Buehner's sisters say that he was born with a pencil in his hand. While he was growing up, pulling out pencils, paper, and watercolors was part of his daily routine. He loved poring over the pictures in books and even used to staple his pictures together to make books. He had no idea that what he was doing would eventually become his career. He grew up to become an award-winning illustrator of books for children. He believes he has the best job in the world!

ISBN-13: 978-0-328-24350-1
ISBN-10:    0-328-24350-7

3 4 5 6 7 8 9 10 V057 16 15 14 13 12 11 10 09 08 07
CC:N1

Dear Reader,

You are about to explore a special street—*Scott Foresman Reading Street.* Are you ready? We hope you'll have fun and that you'll learn new things to share with others. Along the way you will meet some interesting characters. You will meet a boy who has trouble keeping his money. You will read about a lazy bear and a clever hare. You will also meet a girl who helps whales.

As you travel down *Reading Street,* you may read new information that will help you in science and social studies.

While you're enjoying these exciting pieces of literature, we hope you'll find that something else is going on—you are becoming a better reader.

So, put on your walking shoes, and have a great trip!

Sincerely,
The Authors

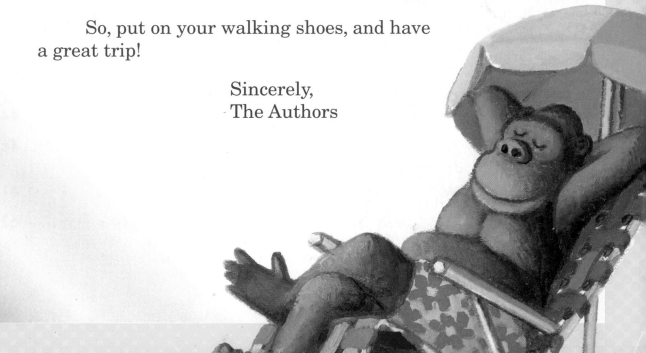

# Dollars and Sense

When is money important, and when does it affect our lives?

4

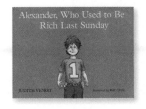

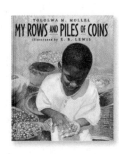

# Smart Solutions

### What are smart ways that problems are solved?

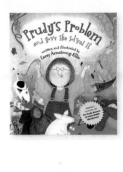

# PEOPLE AND NATURE

## HOW ARE PEOPLE AND NATURE CONNECTED?

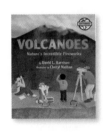

# Dollars and Sense

When is money important, and when does it affect our lives?

11

**Comprehension**

**Skill**
Realism
and Fantasy

**Strategy**
Prior Knowledge

# Realism and Fantasy

- A realistic story tells about something that could happen.

- A fantasy is a story about something that could never happen.

- As you read, ask yourself, "Could this happen?"

| What happens | Could this happen? | This story is a ____. |
|---|---|---|
|  |  |  |

## Strategy: Prior Knowledge

Good readers connect what they are reading with what they already know. Using what you know can help you better understand what you read. You can also use what you know to help you judge whether a story is realistic or a fantasy.

# Write to Read

**1.** Read "Pecos Bill and the Tornado." Make a chart like the one above. Fill it in to help you decide if the story is a realistic story or a fantasy.

**2.** Then write something else Pecos Bill might do. If the story is realistic, add something that could really happen. If the story is a fantasy, add something that could not.

12

# Pecos Bill *and the* TORNADO

Pecos Bill had never fallen off of anything. "I have ridden horses and hogs," Bill said. "I have ridden seahorses and seals. I have even ridden a mountain lion. I have never fallen off of anything!"

One day a big black cloud stormed into town. It was a tornado. The tornado picked up a barn and turned it into a pile of toothpicks! Bill threw his rope around that tornado. Then he hopped on!

**Skill** Here's a clue that this might be a fantasy. Bill couldn't really rope a tornado.

The tornado roared its way across Texas. Bill did not fall off. The tornado picked up a river and shook it back and forth. Now we call it the Snake River. The tornado sucked up a huge chunk of the ground. It's now the Grand Canyon. Still, Bill did not fall off.

**Strategy** What do you know about tornadoes? Use that to help you decide if this is a realistic story or a fantasy.

Bill rode that tornado the whole day. In the end, it became a soft white cloud. Bill hopped off. He was far from Texas. What do you think Bill rode back home?

| |
|---|
| boom |
| pick |
| fetched |
| skillet |
| coins |
| spell |
| business |
| laundry |
| mending |

**Remember**

Try the strategy. Then, if you need more help, use your glossary or a dictionary.

# Vocabulary Strategy
## for Homonyms

**Context Clues** Sometimes when you are reading, you may see a word you know, but the meaning you know doesn't make sense in the sentence. How can that be? The word might be a homonym. Homonyms are words that are pronounced and spelled the same but have different meanings. For example, *bat* means "a stick used to hit a ball." *Bat* also means "a flying animal."

**1.** If a word you know doesn't make sense in the sentence, it might be a homonym.

**2.** Look at the words around it. Can you figure out another meaning?

**3.** Try the new meaning in the sentence. Does it make sense?

As you read "Gold Rush," look for words that are homonyms. Remember to try to figure out another meaning for words that might be homonyms. See which makes sense in the sentence.

14

# GOLD RUSH

In 1848, gold was discovered in California. Thousands of people from all over the world rushed there to look for gold. Many towns became **boom** towns. They grew and grew as more and more people arrived.

But not many people made money by digging for gold. The people who made money were those who sold things to the miners. Tools such as a **pick** and an ax **fetched** a good price. A **skillet** for cooking was worth a stack of **coins**. Miners needed picks and skillets, and these things were hard to find.

After a short **spell** of digging for gold and not finding it, many miners turned to **business**. They found they could make more money doing **laundry** or **mending** clothes. The California gold rush just wasn't all it was cracked up to be.

## Words to Write

Would you have gone off to California to look for gold in 1848? Why or why not? Write your answer. Use words from the Words to Know list.

# Boom Town

by Sonia Levitin
illustrated by
John Sandford

**Genre** **Historical fiction** is a made-up story that takes place in the past. When did this story take place?

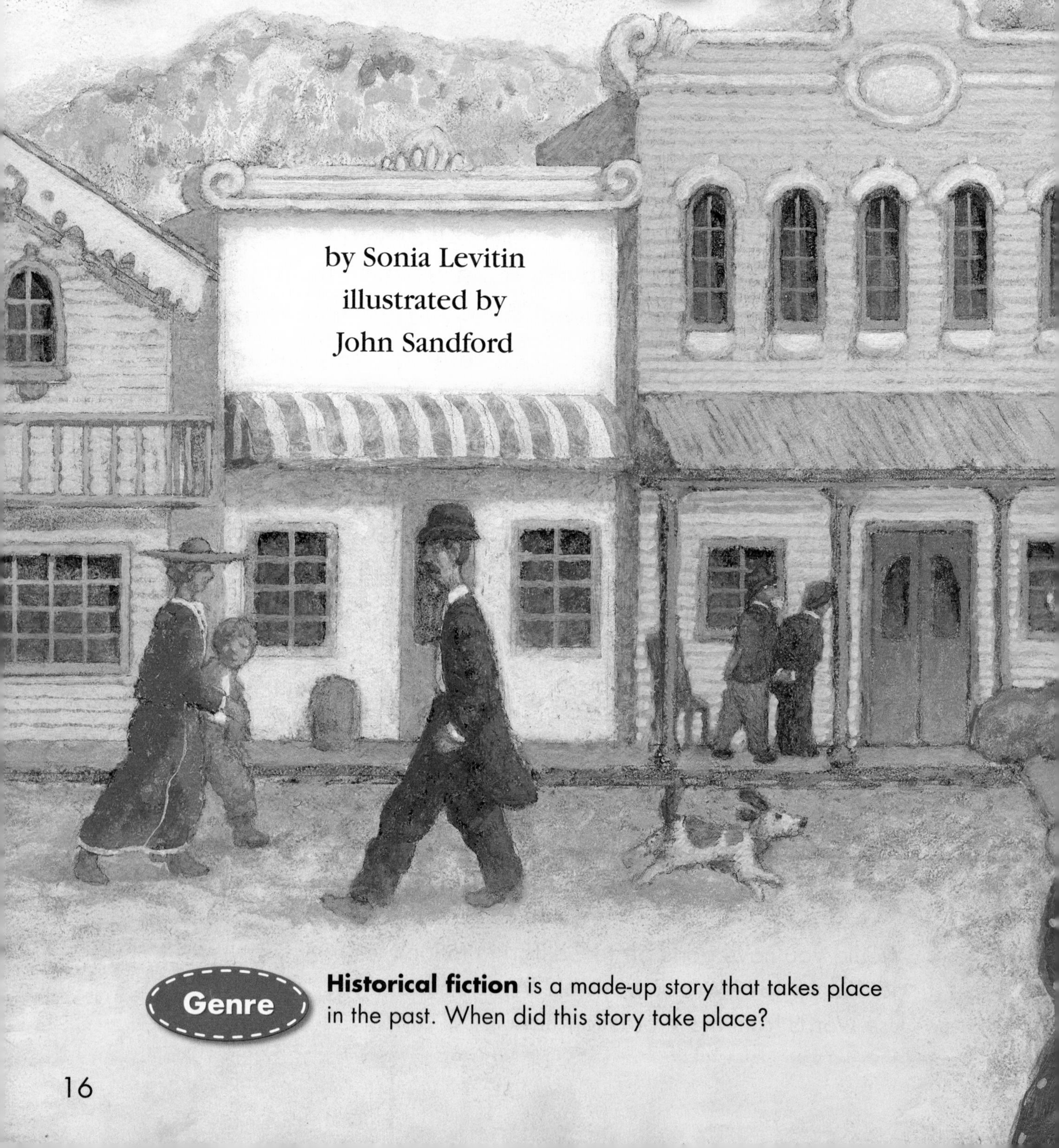

What is a boom town?

It took us twenty-one days on the stagecoach to get to California. When we got there, I thought we'd live with Pa in the gold fields. A whole tent city was built up. But Ma shook her head. "The gold fields are no place for children. We'll get a cabin and live in town."

What town? A stage stop, a pump house, a few log cabins—that was all. It was so wide and lonesome out west, even my shadow ran off.

Ma found a cabin big enough for all of us: Baby Betsy, brothers Billy, Joe, Ted, and me—Amanda. Pa came in from the gold fields every Saturday night, singing:

"So I got me a mule
And some mining tools,
A shovel and a pick and pan;

But I work all day
Without no pay.
I guess I'm a foolish man."

First Ma made him take a bath in a tin tub set out under the stars. Then Pa sang songs and told stories he'd heard from the miners—stories about men finding big nuggets and striking it rich. But poor Pa, he had no luck at all. Still, every Monday morning he'd leave for the gold fields full of hope.

Days were long and lonely. The hills spread out as far as forever. Nights, me and Ma and my brothers and Baby Betsy would sit out and wait for a shooting star to sail across the sky. Once in a while a crow flew by. That's all the excitement there was.

My brothers worked up some furrows.
They planted corn and potatoes and beans.
Then they ran around climbing trees,
skinning their knees. But after all the water
was fetched and the wash was done, after the
soap was made and the fire laid, after the beds
were fixed and the floor was swept clean, I'd
sit outside our cabin door with Baby Betsy, so
bored I thought I'd die. Also, I hankered for
some pie. I loved to bake pie.

I asked Ma and she said, "Pie would be good, but we have no pie pans and no real oven, just the wood stove. How would you bake a pie?"

I poked around in a big box of stuff and found an old iron skillet. I decided to make a pie crust and pick gooseberries to fill it.

Gooseberries grew on the bushes near town. I picked a big pailful and went back home. I made a crust with flour, butter, a little water, and a pinch of salt, and then I rolled it out.

Ma came in and said, "Looks good, Amanda. I knew you could make it. But tell me, how will you bake it?"

I showed Ma the skillet. She shook her head. "I don't think it will work, but you can try."

"It will work," I said.

Brothers Billy and Joe and Ted stood there laughing. When the wood turned to coals, I pushed my pie inside the old stove. After a while I smelled a bad burning. I pulled out my pie, hard as a rock. Billy, Joe, and Ted whooped and slapped their sides.

They snatched up my pie and tossed it high into the air. They ran outside, and Billy whacked it hard with a stick. Pie pieces flew all over the place, and my brothers bent over, laughing.

I was so mad I went right back in to make another, and I swore none of them would get a bite. I rolled out my crust and filled it with berries, shoved the pie into the oven, and soon took it out.

I set the pie down to cool. I went off to do some mending. Next thing I knew, Baby Betsy, just learning to walk, sat there with pie goo all over her face. Too soft, the filling ran down on Betsy, and she wailed like a coyote in the night.

It took one more try, but I got it right. That night we ate my gooseberry pie, and it was delicious.

When Pa came home from the gold fields on Saturday night, there was a pie for him too. "Amanda, you are the queen of the kitchen!" Pa scooped me up and whirled me around. I was proud.

The next week I made an extra pie for Pa to take with him to the gold fields.

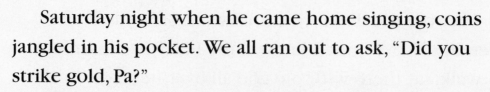

Saturday night when he came home singing, coins
jangled in his pocket. We all ran out to ask, "Did you
strike gold, Pa?"

"No," he said. "I sold Amanda's pie. The miners loved
it. They paid me twenty-five cents a slice!"

After that, Pa took pies to the gold fields every week.
And every week he came home with coins in his
pockets. Some miners walked right to our door
looking for pie. They told Ma, "You should
open a bakery."

Ma said, "It's my girl Amanda who is the
baker. If she wants to make pies, that's fine.
But I have no time."

Ma had a new baby on the way. It was up to me.
I figured I could sell pies to the miners and fill up our
money jar.

But I needed help. I rounded up my brothers and
told them, "If you want to eat pie, you've got to work."

They grumbled and groaned, but they knew I meant
it. So Billy built me a shelf, Joe made a sign, AMANDA'S
FINE PIES, and Ted helped pick berries and sour apples.

I needed more pans and another bucket. One day
Peddler Pete came by, and with the money I'd made
I bought them.

"You're a right smart little girl," said the peddler,
"being in business like this."

I thought fast and told him, "Anybody can
make money out here. Folks need things all the
time, and there're no stores around. If you were to settle
and start one, I'll bet you'd get rich."

Peddler Pete scratched his beard. "Not a bad idea,"
he said. "My feet are sore from roaming. I could use this
cart and build my way up to having a store."

So pretty soon we had us a real store
called PEDDLER PETE'S TRADING POST.
Trappers and traders and travelers
appeared. After shopping at Pete's,
they were good and hungry.

They came to our cabin, looking for pie. Some liked it here so well they decided to stay. Soon we had a cooper, a tanner, a miller, a blacksmith. A town was starting to grow.

A prospector came in on the stage from St. Joe, his clothes covered with dirt. He looked around at the folks eating pie, and he asked, "Is there someone here who does washing?"

I stepped right up and I told him, "What we need is a laundry. Why don't you stay and start one? You'll make more money doing laundry than looking for gold."

The man thought a while, then said with a smile, "You're right, little lady. It's a dandy idea. I'll send for my wife to help."

Soon shirts and sheets fluttered on the line as people brought their washing in. A tailor came to make and mend clothes. A cobbler crafted shoes and boots. We heard the *tap tap* of his hammer and smelled the sweet leather. A barber moved in with shaving mugs and an apothecary with herbs and healing drugs. So the town grew up all around us.

# What About Me?

by Ed Young

Who asks, "What about me?"
and why does he or she ask it?

Once there was a boy who wanted knowledge, but he did not know how to gain it. "I shall see a Grand Master," he said. "He has plenty. Perhaps he will give me some."

When he arrived, he bowed and said, "Grand Master, you are wise. How may I gain a little bit of your knowledge?"

The Grand Master said, "You need to bring me a small carpet for my work." The boy hurried off to find a carpetmaker.

"Carpetmaker," he said, "I need a small carpet to give to the Grand Master for his work."

The carpetmaker barked, "He has needs! What about me? I need thread for weaving my carpets. Bring me some thread, and I will make you a carpet."

**So the boy went off** to find a spinner woman. He found her at last. "Spinner Woman," he said, "I need some thread for the carpetmaker, who will make me a carpet to give to the Grand Master for his work."

"You need thread!" she wheezed. "What about me? I need goat hair to make the thread. Get me some and you can have your thread."

So the boy went off looking for someone who kept goats.

When he came to a goatkeeper, the boy told him his needs. "Your needs! The others' needs! What about me? You need goat hair to buy knowledge–I need goats to provide the hair! Get me some goats, and I will help you."

The boy ran off again to find someone
who sold goats. When he found such a man, the boy
told him of his problems, and the goatseller said,
"What do I know about thread or carpets or Grand
Masters? I need a pen to keep my goats in—they are
straying all over the place! Get me a pen, and you can
have a goat or two."

The boy's head buzzed. "Everyone has a need," he mumbled to himself as he hurried off. "And what of my need for knowledge?" But he went to a carpenter who made pens, and he gave the carpenter his long story.

"Say no more," the carpenter said. "Yes, I make pens, but I need a wife, and no one will have me. Find me a wife, and we can talk about your problems."

So the boy went off, going from house to house.

**Finally** he met a matchmaker. "Yes, I know such a girl–she will make a good wife, but I have a need. All my life, I have wanted. . . . "

"Yes?" said the boy.

"Knowledge," said the matchmaker. "Bring me knowledge, and I will give you the young girl's name to take to the carpenter."

The boy was stunned. "But . . . but we cannot get knowledge without a carpet, no carpet without thread, no thread without hair, no hair without a goat, no goat without a pen, no pen without a wife for the carpenter."

"Stop!" said the matchmaker. "I for one don't want knowledge that bad." And she sent the boy away.

"I need a carpet," the boy chanted. "I need a carpet, I NEED A CARPET!"

And so he began to wander farther and farther from his village.

Until one day he came to a village where he saw a merchant in the marketplace, wringing his hands.

"Merchant," the young man said, "why do you wring your hands?"

The merchant looked at the young man's gentle face. "I have an only and beautiful daughter who I think is mad. I need help, but I don't know where to find it."

"I could not even get a piece of thread when I wanted it," said the young man. "But perhaps I can help."

And so the merchant led him to the girl. When she saw his kind face, she stopped ranting. "Oh, good young man," she said, "I have a need. My father wishes me to marry a merchant like himself, but I love a simple carpenter."

When she described the carpenter, the wanderer suddenly said, "Why, she loves the very carpenter I know!" And so he went to the other village and took the girl and her secret to him.

In thanks, the carpenter immediately gave the young man wood for a pen.

The goatseller placed the goats in the pen and gave him some goats, which he took to the goatkeeper, who gave him some of their hair, which he took to the spinner, who spun him thread.

Then he took the thread to the carpetmaker, who made a small carpet.

This small carpet he carried back to the Grand Master. When he arrived at the house of the wise man, he gave the carpet to him.

"And now, Grand Master, may I have knowledge?"

"But don't you know?" said the Grand Master. "You already have it."

The Grand Master's Morals are Two:

Some of the most precious gifts that we receive are those we receive when we are giving.

and

Often, knowledge comes to us when we least expect it.

# Reader Response

**Open for Discussion** The boy in this story tells about finding knowledge. Do you have a story? Tell a story of how you found knowledge.

**1.** This author makes his own pictures. Look back and find a picture that helps tell the story. Tell how it helps. What does the picture add to the story? **Think Like an Author**

**2.** What is important about the sequence in which this story takes place? **Sequence**

**3.** Summarize, or retell, what happened after the boy met the merchant. **Summarize**

**4.** Draw a map of the boy's journey. Label each stop with the character name plus a new name for the character he visits. For example, instead of Grand Master, label the stop Grand Master/Teacher. **Vocabulary**

**Look Back and Write** The merchant's daughter is important in the story. Look back at page 56. Then explain why she is an important part of the story. Use details from the selection in your answer.

**Meet author and illustrator Ed Young on page 413.**

60

**Prompt**

*What About Me?* tells what happens to a boy as he searches for knowledge. Think about something that has happened to you.
Now write a song about the experience, using a lively voice.

**Writing Trait**

**Voice** shows a writer's style and personality. Use rhyme and repetition to give your song a lively voice.

**Student Model**

Writer speaks directly to reader.

**Guess What Happened**

On my way to the store,
    I found a dime near the shore.
On my way to the store,
    I found a dime.
When I got in the store,
    I dropped my dime on the floor.
When I got in the store,
    I dropped my dime.
When I picked up my dime,
    My left foot slipped on a lime.
When I picked up my dime,
    My left foot slipped.
When I got up off the floor,
    My face was redder than before!

Repetition and rhyme give the song a suitable <u>voice</u>.

The change in the line pattern signals the end of the song.

**Use the model to help you write your own song.**

## Proverbs

### Genre

- Proverbs are short, wise sayings based on common sense.

- Proverbs teach a lesson.

- They have been handed down over many years.

- Many proverbs use old-fashioned language. This is because they were created many years ago.

### Link to Social Studies

Find *Poor Richard's Almanack* in the library. Share other interesting proverbs with your class and explain their meanings. Try to rewrite them using modern language.

# Ben Franklin's Little Words to Live By

by Myka-Lynne Sokoloff

A penny saved is a penny got.

An egg today is better than a hen tomorrow.

He that waits upon fortune, is never sure of a dinner.

Early to bed and early to rise makes a man healthy, wealthy, and wise.

– Ben Franklin

**D**o you know any of these sayings? Short, catchy ideas like these are called proverbs. These sayings are meant to teach a lesson.

The proverbs on this page are all alike in two ways. First, they teach lessons about money or greed. Second, they all come from Ben Franklin.

In the 1700s, Ben Franklin wrote little books called *Poor Richard's Almanack*. The books are filled with proverbs that teach lessons Franklin thought people should learn. He believed in using money wisely and working hard. Franklin tried to practice these lessons himself.

Ben Franklin did many things besides writing his *Almanack*. He started a hospital and a library. He invented reading glasses. Franklin also helped with ideas for the Declaration of Independence.

Take another look at Franklin's proverbs. Think about what they mean. Which one teaches an important lesson *you* could learn?

## Reading Across Texts

*What About Me?* and Ben Franklin's proverbs all teach lessons. How are the lessons alike, and how are they different?

**Writing Across Texts**
Choose a proverb. Then think about *What About Me?* Write a short paragraph comparing the two lessons you learned.

**⊙ Summarize**  Sum up what you read about Ben Franklin.

63

**Comprehension**

**Skill**
Sequence

**Strategy**
Visualize

_Skill_

# Sequence

- Sequence is the order in which things happen in a story. As you read, pay attention to what happens first, next, and last.

- Sometimes a writer uses clue words like *then*, *next*, and *finally*.

**First Event**          **Next Event**

**Second Event**          **Last Event**

_Strategy_

## Strategy: Visualize

Active readers make pictures in their minds as they read a story. As you read, picture in your mind the characters and what is happening. That will help you keep track of the sequence of events.

# Write to Read

**1.** Read "Inez's Birthday Gift." Make a time line like the one above. Note the sequence of events. List as many events as you need to.

**2.** Write a description of how you pictured Inez when her grandmother gave her the birthday money *and* when she looked at the price tag on the camera.

# Inez's Birthday Gift

Inez's grandmother gave Inez money for her birthday. Now Inez could buy the camera she'd been wanting!

The next day, Inez and her grandmother walked to the camera shop. Just inside the door Inez saw a camera bag. It was blue with butterflies on it. Inez loved butterflies. She picked up the bag. Then she saw a camera strap. It was the same color blue as the camera bag. Inez picked up the strap. Next, she saw photo albums. One had a butterfly picture on it. It was perfect! Inez picked up that too.

Finally, Inez walked over to the camera she wanted. She looked at the price tag on the camera. If she bought the bag, the strap, and the album, she would not have enough money to buy the camera!

Inez sighed and put everything back. Then she picked up the camera and followed her grandmother to the checkout counter.

**Skill** Here is the first thing that happens to Inez. You could add this to a time line.

**Strategy** Here's a good place to stop and visualize. What do you see in your mind as you think about Inez carrying all these things?

65

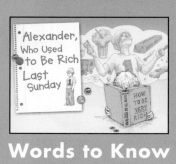

## Words to Know

| |
|---|
| college |
| rich |
| downtown |
| nickels |
| dimes |
| quarters |
| fined |

# Vocabulary Strategy
## for Unfamiliar Words

**Glossary or Dictionary** You can use a glossary or a dictionary to find the meaning of a word you don't know. A glossary appears at the back of a book and lists important words from that book and their meanings. A dictionary is a separate book that lists words and their meanings, as well as other information about the words. The words in a glossary or a dictionary are listed in alphabetical order.

**1.** Look at the first letter in the word.

**2.** Turn to the section for that letter in the glossary or dictionary.

**3.** Read the entry for the word. If the word has more than one meaning, decide which meaning you think fits in the sentence.

**4.** Try that meaning in the sentence to see if it makes sense.

As you read "Saving Money," use a glossary or a dictionary to find the meanings of the vocabulary words.

# SAVING MONEY

What do you want to be when you grow up? Maybe you want to be a teacher, a veterinarian, or an astronaut. To get the job you want, you may need to go to college. College costs a lot of money. You do not have to be rich to go, but you will need to save money.

Saving money is hard. When you go downtown or to the mall, there are many wonderful things you can buy—books, CDs, video games. How can you do it? Perhaps relatives give you money on your birthday and at holidays. Perhaps family members or neighbors pay you to do extra chores. Try to put half of any money you get in your bank. Remember, the nickels, dimes, and quarters you save will add up very quickly.

Before you know it, you'll need a bigger bank. And even if the rule in your house is that you're fined ten cents for not making your bed or for teasing your little sister, you'll be able to afford it. But don't make it a habit if you want to go to college.

## Words to Write

Write about what you do to earn money. Think of other things you can do. Write about them too. Use words from the Words to Know list.

# Alexander, Who Used to Be Rich Last Sunday

by Judith Viorst

illustrated by Ray Cruz

 **Genre**   **Realistic fiction** is a made-up story that could really happen. Do you know anyone like Alexander?

Why isn't Alexander rich now?

It isn't fair that my brother Anthony has two dollars and three quarters and one dime and seven nickels and eighteen pennies.

It isn't fair that my brother Nicholas has one dollar and two quarters and five dimes and five nickels and thirteen pennies.

It isn't fair because what I've got is . . . bus tokens.

And most of the time what I've mostly got is . . . bus tokens.

And even when I'm very rich, I know that pretty soon what I'll have is . . . bus tokens.

I know because I used to be rich.

Last Sunday.

Last Sunday Grandma Betty and Grandpa Louie came to visit from New Jersey. They brought lox because my father likes to eat lox. They brought plants because my mother likes to grow plants. They brought a dollar for me and a dollar for Nick and a dollar for Anthony because—Mom says it isn't nice to say this—we like money.

A lot. Especially me.

# How Many Pennies?

Psst

The sign on the jar in the store read, "Guess the number of pennies and WIN them!" Jason looked at the jar. He didn't know how to guess. He started to walk away when he heard, "*Psst.*" Jason didn't see anyone. "*Psst.*"

"Hey, kid," said the jar. The jar was talking, and to him! It said, "Come closer, and I'll tell you how many pennies are inside me."

Jason wrote down the number the jar said and put it in the box for guesses. On Saturday, he returned to hear his name announced as the winner! Jason took the jar home and dumped the pennies out on his bed. "What am I going to do with all these pennies?" he said to himself.

"*Psst.*" Jason looked around. He didn't see anyone. "*Psst.* Hey, kid," said his bed. "Come closer, and I'll tell you what you should buy with these pennies."

**Skill** So far, this story seems realistic. This could really happen.

**Strategy** If you are not sure about what you have just read, this would be a good spot to stop and reread.

Psst

87

| amount |
|---|
| worth |
| value |
| earned |
| interest |
| expensive |
| check |
| thousand |
| million |

**Remember**

Try the strategy. Then, if you need more help, use your glossary or a dictionary.

# Vocabulary Strategy
## for Multiple-Meaning Words

**Context Clues** Sometimes during reading, you may come across a word whose meaning doesn't make sense. The word might have another meaning. For example, *band* means "a musical group." But it also means "a strip of material." The words around the unknown word may help you figure out another meaning.

**1.** If you come to a word that doesn't make sense, think about another meaning.

**2.** Look at nearby words or sentences. Can you figure out another meaning?

**3.** Try the new meaning in the sentence. Does it make sense?

As you read "Money," look for words that can have more than one meaning. Look at the nearby words to figure out the meaning that makes sense.

We use money every day, so it is important to understand money. Are two dimes the same amount of money as four nickels? Are twenty nickels worth one dollar? What is the value of two five-dollar bills? If these sound like math questions, well, they are. Money is based on numbers.

Have you ever earned money by working? You can earn even more when you put that money in a bank. The bank uses the money, and it pays people for using their money. The money the bank pays is called interest.

When people buy something expensive, they often write a check. If a woman buys a used car for $1,000, she might write a check and give it to the seller. The check tells the woman's bank to take $1,000 from her money and give it to the seller's bank to add to his money. That's easier (and safer) than carrying a thousand dollars. What if someone were buying something for a million dollars? A check would be much more convenient.

## Words to Write

Think of something spectacular that you would like to buy. Tell about it and what you could do to earn the money to buy it. Use as many words from the Words to Know list as you can.

**Genre**

**Nonfiction** text explains something about real life. What do you expect to learn from this selection?

90

# CONGRATULATIONS! YOU'VE EARNED A PENNY.

ONE PENNY

It will buy anything that costs one cent.

## WELL DONE! YOU'VE MADE A NICKEL.

ONE NICKEL

is worth the same as FIVE PENNIES.

## HOORAY! NOW YOU HAVE A DIME.

ONE DIME

has the same value as TWO NICKELS

or TEN PENNIES.

93

# EXCELLENT! FOR YOUR HARD WORK YOU'VE EARNED A QUARTER.

ONE QUARTER

is the same amount of money as FIVE NICKELS

or TWO DIMES AND ONE NICKEL

or THREE NICKELS AND ONE DIME

or TWENTY-FIVE PENNIES.

BLOW UP this BOA Earn 25¢

94

# WONDERFUL! YOU ARE NOW A DOLLAR RICHER.

ONE DOLLAR

is worth as much as
FOUR QUARTERS . . .

FIX THIS
FOUNTAIN'S FLOW
Earn $1.

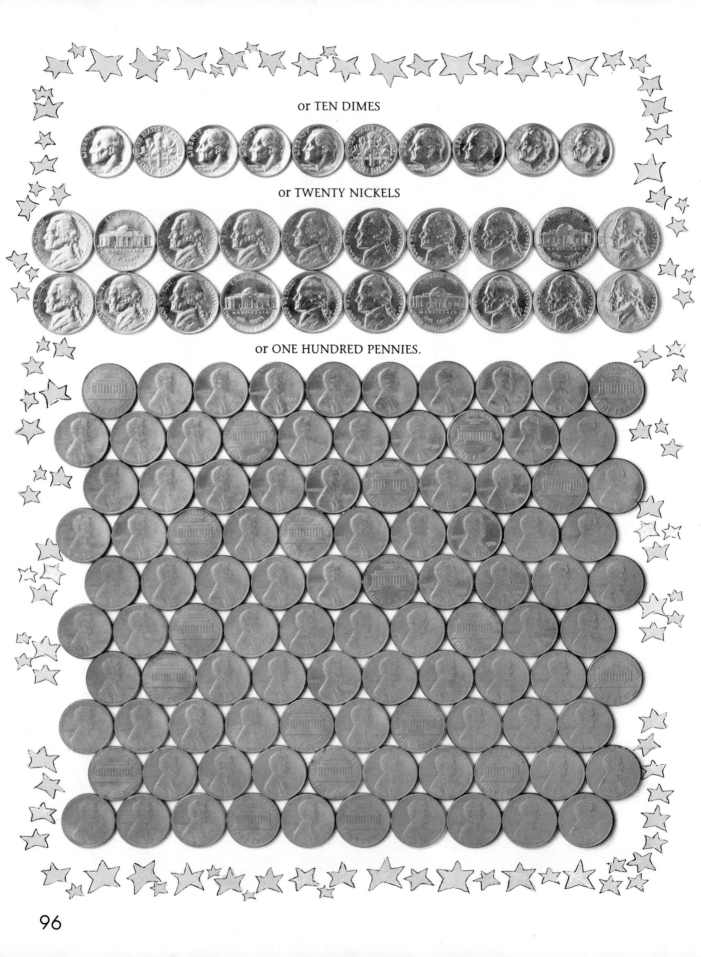

or TEN DIMES

or TWENTY NICKELS

or ONE HUNDRED PENNIES.

You could use your dollar to buy one hundred pieces of penny candy, or twenty five-cent balloons, or ten stickers for ten cents each, or four rubber balls that cost twenty-five cents apiece.

Or perhaps you'd like to save your dollar. You could put it in the bank, and a year from now it will be worth $1.05.

The bank wants to use your money, and it will pay you five cents to leave your dollar there for a year. The extra five cents is called interest.

If you waited ten years, your dollar would earn sixty-four cents in interest just from sitting in the bank.

Are you interested in earning lots of interest? Wait twenty years, and one dollar will grow to $2.70.

**DELICIOUS! YOU'VE BAKED A CAKE AND EARNED FIVE DOLLARS.**

You could be paid with one five-dollar bill or
five one-dollar bills. It doesn't matter. They have the
same value.

## STUPENDOUS! YOU'VE MADE TEN DOLLARS.

How would you like to be paid?

One ten-dollar bill? Two five-dollar bills? Ten one-dollar bills? Or perhaps one five and five ones? Take your pick—they're all worth ten dollars.

or

or

If you prefer coins, you can have a five-foot stack of pennies (that's one thousand of them) or a fifteen-inch stack of two hundred nickels. You could also be paid with one hundred dimes, which would stack up to just over five inches. Or you can receive your ten dollars as a 3 1/4-inch pile of forty quarters.

You could spend your ten dollars on ten kittens or one thousand kitty snacks.

Or you could take your mom to the movies.

But maybe you'd rather save your money. If you leave your ten dollars in the bank for ten years, it will earn $6.40 in interest, and you will have $16.40.

If you leave it there for fifty years, your ten dollars will grow to $138.02.

**YOU'VE WORKED HARD TO EARN ONE HUNDRED DOLLARS.** You've decided to spend it on a plane ticket to the beach. You could pay with a hundred-dollar bill, or two fifty-dollar bills, or five twenty-dollar bills, or many other combinations—six fives, three tens, and two twenties, for instance.

Paying with pennies? You'll need ten thousand of them, and they'll make a fifty-foot stack.

## YOU'VE WORKED LONG AND HARD, AND YOU'VE EARNED A THOUSAND DOLLARS!

You're going to buy a pet. You could pay with coins or bills.

If you don't like the idea of carrying a thousand dollars around with you, you can put it in the bank and pay for the hippo with a check. The check tells your bank to give $1,000 to the person who sold you the hippo.

Here's how it works: You give the check to the person who sold you the hippo, and he gives it to his bank, and his bank sends it to a very busy clearinghouse in the city, and the clearinghouse tells your bank to take $1,000 out of your money.

After your bank does that, the clearinghouse tells the hippo salesman's bank to add $1,000 to his money, so he can take it and use it whenever, and however, he likes. Maybe he'll use it to raise more hippos.

If you used pennies to purchase a $10,000 Ferris wheel, someone might not be too happy about it. Even if you used ten thousand one-dollar bills, they would be mighty hard to handle.

Probably a check would be best.

## MAGNIFICENT! YOU'VE EARNED $50,000.

And you've just read about a well-worn, unloved, but perfectly fixable castle for sale. The price: $100,000.

The castle costs $100,000 and you have only $50,000. You're $50,000 short, but you can still buy the castle. You could use the money you earned as a down payment and ask a bank to lend you the rest.

Then you would pay the bank back, a little at a time, month after month . . . for many years.

But the amount you must pay the bank will be *more* than what you borrowed. That's because the bank charges for lending you money. The extra money is called interest, just like the interest the bank pays to you when it uses your money. Now you are using the bank's money, so you must pay interest to the bank.

If you have some very expensive plans, you may have to take on a tough job that pays well.

If you think ogre-taming would be an exciting challenge, you can have fun and make a great deal of money too. Of course, you may not enjoy taming obstreperous ogres or building bulky bridges or painting purple pots. Enjoying your work is more important than money, so you should look for another job or make less expensive plans.

# CONGRATULATIONS! YOU'VE MADE A MILLION.

## A MILLION DOLLARS!

That's a stack of pennies ninety-five miles high, or enough nickels to fill a school bus, or a whale's weight in quarters.

Would you prefer your million in paper money? Even a paper million is a hefty load: A million one-dollar bills would weigh 2,500 pounds and stack up to 360 feet.

What's the smallest your million could be? One-hundred-dollar bills are the largest made today, and it would take ten thousand of them to pay you for your feat of ogre-taming. But a check for $1,000,000 would easily fit in your pocket or purse. And it's worth the same as the towering stacks of pennies or bills.

Now you can afford to buy tickets to the moon. Or you can purchase some real estate for the endangered rhinoceroses.

But if you'd rather save your million than spend it, you could put it in the bank, where it would earn interest. The interest on a million is about $1,000 a week, or $143 a day, or $6 an hour, or 10 cents a minute. Just from sitting in the bank!

If you keep your million, you can probably live on the interest without doing any more work for the rest of your life. You might like that, or you could find it rather dull. Making money means making choices.

**SO WHAT WOULD YOU DO IF YOU MADE A MILLION?**

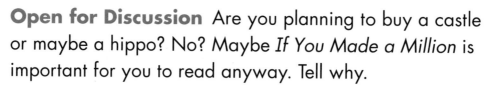

# Reader Response

**Open for Discussion** Are you planning to buy a castle or maybe a hippo? No? Maybe *If You Made a Million* is important for you to read anyway. Tell why.

**1.** The author couldn't tell everything, so the artist wrote some things in his pictures. Read the words in the pictures. Why are they there? **Think Like an Author**

**2.** How is this selection different from other nonfiction selections you have read? Talk about whether you like it, and tell why or why not. **Realism and Fantasy**

**3.** Did you need to reread any part of the selection? How did that help you? What else could you have done? **Monitor and Fix Up**

**4.** Tell what you would do if you made a million dollars. Use words from the Words to Know list. **Vocabulary**

 **Look Back and Write** Look back at page 106. What is more important than money? Use details from the selection in your answer.

Meet author **David M. Schwartz on page 418 and** illustrator **Steven Kellogg on page 420.**

110

# Write Now

## Prompt

*If You Made a Million* suggests ways you could spend different amounts of money. Think about how you would spend $100. Now write an e-mail to a friend explaining what you would do.

### Writing Trait

Use your purpose for writing to help you **focus** on your main **idea.**

**Student Model**

**You can use contractions in an informal e-mail to a friend.**

**Sentence states the main idea.**

To: Travis McCrae

From: Jacob Grunberg

Can you believe it? I've earned $100 dog-walking! Here's what I'm going to do with the money. I'll buy some garden plants for Mom for Mother's Day. Then I'll get the new Blaster video game for Russell for his birthday. Next I'll replace Cindy's doll cradle. I fell on it when we were playing catch, remember? I should have enough money left to buy summer passes to Water World for you and me. What do you think of my plan?

**Most sentences <u>focus</u> on one idea—how the writer plans to spend the money.**

**Use the model to help you write your own e-mail.**

111

### Picture Encyclopedia

#### Genre

- Picture encyclopedias provide information on a variety of topics.
- The information is in both written and picture format.
- A reader may read the information in any order.

#### Text Features

- Headings tell what each section will be about.
- Labels identify each picture.

#### Link to Social Studies

Use the library and learn about the money used in a country of your choice. What is the money called? What is it made of? Share what you find with the class.

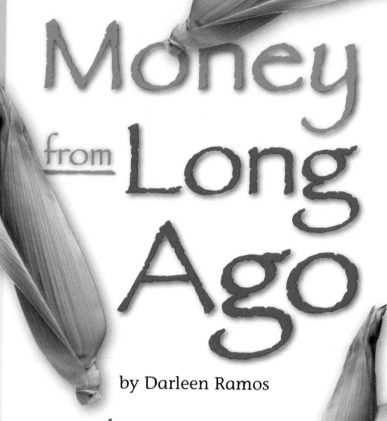

# Money from Long Ago

by Darleen Ramos

## Introduction

In ancient times, people did not use paper money or coins. They traded to get things they needed. A person might trade three ears of corn for five potatoes. A farmer might trade a sheep for several chickens.

If the trade was not even, people used other things for payment. They may have used beans, shells, furs, or tools. Here are a few items people used as money.

## Cowrie Shells

Cowries are small snails that live in the ocean. In ancient times, their shiny shells were used as money in China, India, and parts of Africa. The shells are one of the oldest forms of payment. Cowrie shells could be stored or worn. The color and size of the shell would set its price.

**Cowrie shells**

## Feather Coils

Before there were coins and paper money, the people on the Pacific island of Santa Cruz used a feather coil for money. The coil was made from the red feathers of a honey-eating bird. The feathers were glued on the coil, which is about ten yards long. Red feather money was used in marriage contracts and to buy boats.

**Red feather money coil**

 **Monitor and Fix-Up** If you're confused, try reading on.

## Salt Bar

Hundreds of years ago, people from Africa and China used salt as money. Pure salt was expensive. Salt was used to keep food from going bad. The salt was cut into standard sizes and covered in reeds. This protected the salt from breaking. It also kept people from scratching off some of the salt between trades.

**Reed protecting a salt bar**

## Stone Discs

Long ago, the people from Yap, an island in the Pacific, used large stone discs as money. The stones had holes in the middle. The giant discs were not moved when paid to a new owner. That's because the largest stones weighed over 400 pounds! People used the stone discs to arrange marriages and to trade houses or boats.

**Stone disc**

# Wampum

Centuries ago, Native Americans used a belt of beads for trading. This wampum was made from clam shells that were smoothed into beads. Each belt was special. The bead maker used different colors and patterns. Wampum belts were also traded during peace agreements.

**Wampum belt**

## Reading Across Texts

What makes paper money and coins easier to use than the money from long ago, such as shells, feather coils, salt, stones, and beads?

**Writing Across Texts** Make a chart. List the "good" and the "bad" of each kind of money.

**Monitor and Fix-Up**   If something doesn't make sense, try rereading.

**Comprehension**

**Skill**
Character
and Setting

**Strategy**
Story Structure

# Character and Setting

- A character is a person who takes part in the events of a story.

- Writers tell some things about characters. You can also figure out about characters by their words and actions.

- The setting is when and where a story takes place.

- A writer may tell you the setting, or you may figure out the setting from details.

| Story Title | |
|---|---|
| Characters | Setting |

## Strategy: Story Structure

A story has a beginning, a middle, and an end. This means that events happen all along the way. One event leads to the next. Good readers use this structure to learn about the characters and the setting.

## Write to Read

**1.** Read "Saturday Is Market Day." Make a chart like the one above. Write details from the story that tell about the main character and the setting.

**2.** Write a paragraph that tells the main events of "Saturday Is Market Day" in the order in which they happened.

# Saturday Is Market Day

We got up before the sun to make the trip into town. My family lives in a little village in Africa. Every Saturday we go to town to sell our head scarves. Mama makes the scarves. Sometimes I help. They are the very best scarves you could buy.

Papa pulled the cart into the market as the sun came up. My sister Fusi and I laid out the scarves. We ate breakfast before our first customer came.

It was not long before we sold our first scarves. A woman and her daughter bought them. Soon we began to sell many more.

At ten, drummers set up near us. As they played, Papa and Fusi danced. Mama and I clapped along.

In the afternoon, one customer had me turn around and around. She was looking at the scarf I was wearing. I had made it myself. She bought my scarf!

It was a good market day. I am looking forward to next Saturday.

**MY ROWS AND PILES OF COINS**

## Words to Know

errands

bundles

steady

wobbled

dangerously

arranged

unwrapped

excitedly

**Remember**

Try the strategy. Then, if you need more help, use your glossary or a dictionary.

# Vocabulary Strategy
## for Prefixes and Suffixes

**Word Structure** When you see a word you don't know, look closely at the word. Does it have *un-* at the beginning? Does it have *-ly* at the end? The prefix *un-* makes a word mean "not ____" or "the opposite of ____." For example, *unhappy* means "not happy."

The suffix *-ly* makes a word mean "in a ____ way." For example, *slowly* means "in a slow way." You can use *un-* or *-ly* to help you figure out the meaning of a word.

**1.** Put your finger over the prefix or suffix.

**2.** Look at the base word. (That's the word without the prefix or suffix.) Put the base word in an appropriate phrase:

"the opposite of ____" for *un-*

"in a ____ way" for *-ly*.

**3.** Try that meaning in the sentence. Does it make sense?

Read "A Gift for Cletus." Look for words that begin with *un-* or end with *-ly*. Use the prefix or suffix to help you figure out the meanings of the words.

# A GIFT FOR CLETUS

Every Saturday Cletus ran errands for his neighbors to earn money. They gave him lists of things to buy in town. They gave him bundles to drop off. Sometimes Cletus had so much piled on the front of his bike that he could not keep the bike steady. He wobbled dangerously from side to side, and the bundles would almost fall into the street. Cletus had to ride very slowly, keeping one hand on the bundles.

Cletus wanted to buy a big basket for the back of his bike. He knew that with the bundles arranged behind him, it would be easier and safer to ride back and forth to town. But he had not saved enough money yet.

The neighbors really appreciated what Cletus did for them. They wanted a way to say *thank you*. So they all got together and bought Cletus a basket for his bike. He unwrapped the gift and excitedly put the new basket on his bike. He thanked his neighbors, and then off he went again with their lists and bundles.

## Words to Write

Now what do you think Cletus should save his money for? Write your ideas. Use words from the Words to Know list.

# MY ROWS AND PILES OF COINS

by Tololwa M. Mollel

illustrated by E.B. Lewis

Why does the boy put his coins into piles and rows?

121

After a good day at the market, my mother, Yeyo, gave me five whole ten-cent coins. I gaped at the money until Yeyo nudged me. "Saruni, what are you waiting for? Go and buy yourself something."

I plunged into the market. I saw roasted peanuts, *chapati,* rice cakes, and *sambusa.* There were wooden toy trucks, kites, slingshots, and marbles. My heart beat excitedly. I wanted to buy everything, but I clutched my coins tightly in my pocket.

At the edge of the market, I stopped. In a neat sparkling row stood several big new bicycles. One of them was decorated all over with red and blue.

That's what I would buy!

For some time now, Murete, my father, had been teaching me to ride his big, heavy bicycle. If only I had a bicycle of my own!

A gruff voice startled me. "What are you looking for, little boy?"

I turned and bumped into a tall skinny man, who laughed at my confusion. Embarrassed, I hurried back to Yeyo.

That night, I dropped five ten-cent coins into my
secret money box. It held other ten-cent coins Yeyo had
given me for helping with market work on Saturdays.
By the dim light of a lantern, I feasted my eyes on the
money. I couldn't believe it was all mine.

I emptied the box, arranged all the coins in piles
and the piles in rows. Then I counted the coins and
thought about the bicycle I longed to buy.

Every day after school, when I wasn't helping
Yeyo to prepare supper, I asked Murete if I could ride
his bicycle. He held the bicycle steady while I rode
around, my toes barely touching the pedals.

Whenever Murete let go, I wobbled, fell off, or
crashed into things and among coffee trees. Other
children from the neighborhood had a good laugh
watching me.

*Go on, laugh,* I thought, sore but determined.
Soon I would be like a cheetah on wheels, racing on
errands with my very own bicycle!

Saturday after Saturday, we took goods to market, piled high on Yeyo's head and on my squeaky old wooden wheelbarrow. We sold dried beans and maize, pumpkins, spinach, bananas, firewood, and eggs.

My money box grew heavier.

I emptied the box, arranged the coins in piles and the piles in rows. Then I counted the coins and thought about the blue and red bicycle.

After several more lessons Murete let me ride on my own while he shouted instructions. *"Eyes up, arms straight, keep pedaling, slow down!"* I enjoyed the breeze on my face, the pedals turning smoothly under my feet, and, most of all, Yeyo's proud smile as she watched me ride. How surprised she would be to see my new bicycle! And how grateful she would be when I used it to help her on market days!

The heavy March rains came. The ground became so muddy, nobody went to market. Instead, I helped Yeyo with house chores. When it wasn't raining, I helped Murete on the coffee farm. We pruned the coffee trees and put fallen leaves and twigs around the coffee stems. Whenever I could, I practiced riding Murete's bicycle.

It stopped raining in June. Not long after, school closed. Our harvest—fresh maize and peas, sweet potatoes, vegetables, and fruits—was so big, we went to market on Saturdays *and* Wednesdays. My money box grew heavier and heavier.

I emptied the box, arranged the coins in piles and the piles in rows. Then I counted the coins and thought about the bicycle I would buy.

A few days later I grew confident enough to try to ride a loaded bicycle. With Murete's help, I strapped a giant pumpkin on the carrier behind me. When I attempted to pedal, the bicycle wobbled so dangerously that Murete, alongside me, had to grab it.

All right, Sarufi, the load is too heavy for you," he said, and I got off. Mounting the bicycle to ride back to the house, he sighed wearily. "And hard on my bones, which are getting too old for pedaling."

I practiced daily with smaller loads, and slowly I learned to ride a loaded bicycle. No more pushing the squeaky old wheelbarrow, I thought. I would ride with my load tall and proud on my bicycle—just like Murete!

On the first Saturday after school opened in July, we went to market as usual. Late in the afternoon, after selling all we had, Yeyo sat talking with another trader.

I set off into the crowd. I wore an old coat Murete had handed down to me for chilly July days like today. My precious coins were wrapped in various bundles inside the oversize pockets of the coat.

*I must be the richest boy in the world,* I thought, feeling like a king. *I can buy anything.*

The tall skinny man was polishing his bicycles as I came up. "I want to buy a bicycle," I said, and brought out my bundles of coins.

The man whistled in wonder as I unwrapped the money carefully on his table. "How many coins have you got there?"

Proudly, I told him. "Three hundred and five."

"Three hundred and . . . five," he muttered. "Mmh, that's . . . thirty shillings and fifty cents." He exploded with laughter. "A whole bicycle . . . for thirty shillings . . . and fifty cents?"

His laugh followed me as I walked away with my bundles of coins, deeply disappointed.

On our way home, Yeyo asked what was wrong.
I had to tell her everything.

"You saved all your money for a bicycle to help me?"
she asked. I could tell she was amazed and touched.
"How nice of you!" As for the tall skinny man, she
scoffed, "*Oi!* What does he know? Of course you will
buy a bicycle. One day you will."

Her kind words did not cheer me.

The next afternoon, the sound of a
*pikipiki* filled the air, *tuk-tuk-tuk-tuk-tuk.*
I came out of the house and stared in
astonishment. Murete was perched on
an orange motorbike.

He cut the engine and dismounted. Then,
chuckling at my excited questions about the
*pikipiki,* he headed into the house.

When Murete came out, Yeyo was with him, and
he was wheeling his bicycle. "I want to sell this to you.
For thirty shillings and fifty cents." He winked at me.

Surprised, I stared at Murete. How did he know
about my secret money box? I hadn't told him anything.

Then suddenly, I realized the wonderful thing
that had just happened. "My bicycle, I have my very
own bicycle!" I said, and it didn't matter at all that it
wasn't decorated with red and blue. Within moments,
I had brought Murete my money box.

Murete gave Yeyo the box. Yeyo, in turn, gave it to me. Puzzled, I looked from Yeyo to Murete and to Yeyo again. "You're giving it . . . back to me?"

Yeyo smiled. "It's a reward for all your help to us."

"Thank you, thank you!" I cried gleefully.

The next Saturday, my load sat tall and proud on my bicycle, which I walked importantly to market. I wasn't riding it because Yeyo could never have kept up.

Looking over at Yeyo, I wished she didn't have to carry such a big load on her head.

*If only I had a cart to pull behind my bicycle,* I thought, *I could lighten her load!*

That night I emptied the box, arranged all the coins in piles and the piles in rows. Then I counted the coins and thought about the cart I would buy. . . .

File    Edit    View    Favorites    Tools    Help

http://www.

# A Money Web Site

**Want to save money and make it grow?
Click on a link and find out how.**

Open a Savings Account

Save as You Spend

Buy Savings Bonds

Let's say you need a plan, so you click here.

**Text Structure**    How do you decide what to read first?

If you click on <u>Save as You Spend</u>, you might see the following.

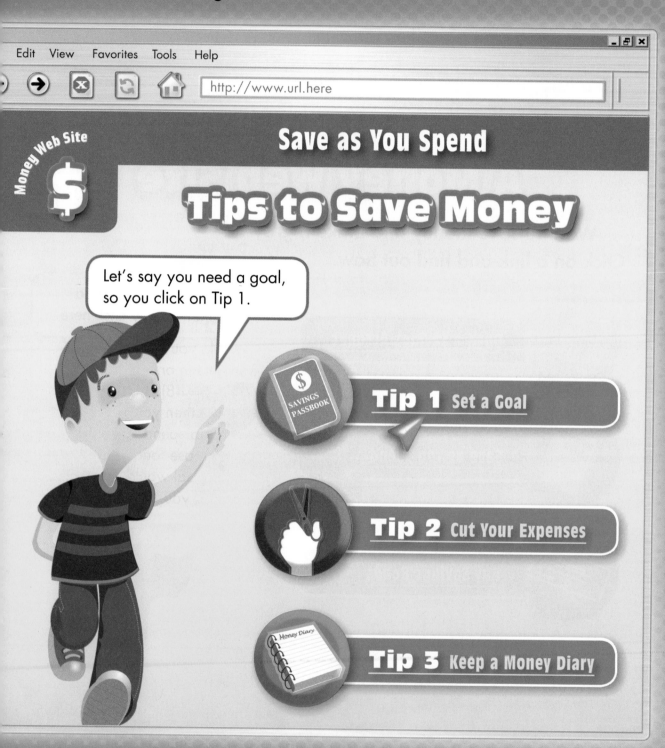

Edit   View   Favorites   Tools   Help

http://www.url.here

**Money Web Site**

# Save as You Spend

## Tips to Save Money

Let's say you need a goal, so you click on Tip 1.

**Tip 1** Set a Goal

**Tip 2** Cut Your Expenses

**Tip 3** Keep a Money Diary

**Prior Knowledge**   What do you know that helped you decide where to click?

140

If you click on <u>Tip 1 Set a Goal</u>, you will find this information.

## Set a Goal

Money Web Site

Suppose your goal is a new pair of sneakers that costs $48, and you earn $12 a week mowing lawns. What's your plan? How quickly do you want those sneakers?

**Plan 1** If you save $6 a week, it will take you eight weeks to save enough to buy them (6 x 8 = 48). Are you patient enough to wait nearly two months?

**Plan 2** If you save $12 a week, you can buy the sneakers in only four weeks (4 x 12 = 48). That's twice as fast! But then you won't have any extra spending money during those four weeks. Which goal would you set? It's up to you.

### Reading Across Texts

Which method of saving does Saruni follow in saving for a bike, Plan 1 or Plan 2?

**Writing Across Texts** In a letter to Saruni, explain the method he chose.

# A Single Penny

by Felice Holman

A single penny
does not jingle
in my pocket,
but two would
make a single
jingle
and would do.
And three
would be
a real
tympani!

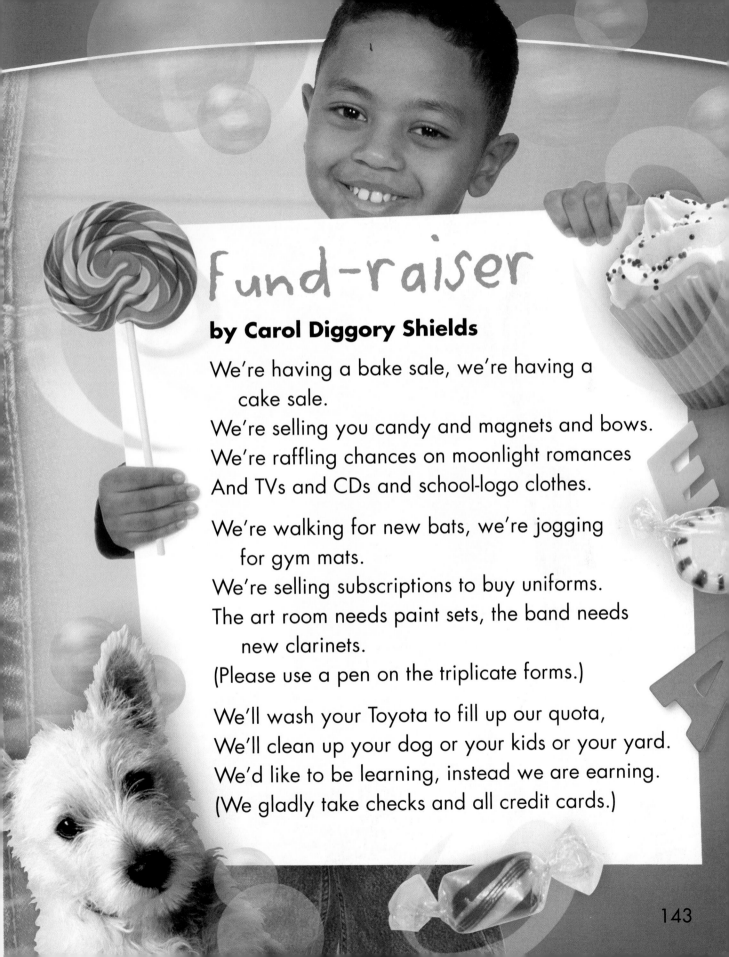

# Fund-raiser

**by Carol Diggory Shields**

We're having a bake sale, we're having a
    cake sale.
We're selling you candy and magnets and bows.
We're raffling chances on moonlight romances
And TVs and CDs and school-logo clothes.

We're walking for new bats, we're jogging
    for gym mats.
We're selling subscriptions to buy uniforms.
The art room needs paint sets, the band needs
    new clarinets.
(Please use a pen on the triplicate forms.)

We'll wash your Toyota to fill up our quota,
We'll clean up your dog or your kids or your yard.
We'd like to be learning, instead we are earning.
(We gladly take checks and all credit cards.)

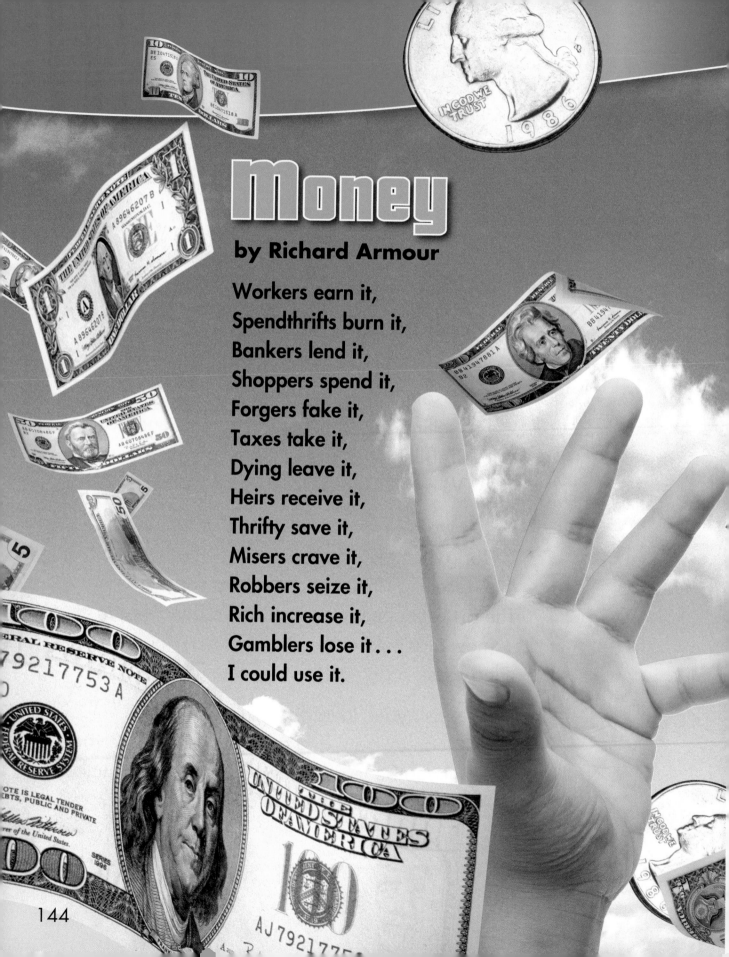

# Money

**by Richard Armour**

Workers earn it,
Spendthrifts burn it,
Bankers lend it,
Shoppers spend it,
Forgers fake it,
Taxes take it,
Dying leave it,
Heirs receive it,
Thrifty save it,
Misers crave it,
Robbers seize it,
Rich increase it,
Gamblers lose it . . .
I could use it.

# Coins

**by Valerie Worth**

Coins are pleasant
To the hand:

Neat circles, smooth,
A little heavy.

They feel as if
They are worth something.

## MAKING MY FORTUNE

connect to
**WRITING**

In *Boom Town,* you learned how one smart girl used her skills to open a successful business that helped build a town. Think of a special skill or talent that you have. How could you use it to offer a product or a service that people would buy? Write a paragraph or more telling how you could use your skill to open a business.

My Special Skills

## FEEL LIKE A MILLIONAIRE

You learned about the value of money in several selections in this unit. In *Alexander, Who Used to Be Rich Last Sunday,* Alexander explains exactly what happened to the dollar he got. Suppose someone gave you 100 dollars. Make a budget to show how you might use the money. Spend the money on at least seven different things. Your total should add up to 100 dollars.

## GREAT DEBATE

In *What About Me?*, the main character searched for knowledge, while other characters wanted things. Form two debate teams. One team will argue that things are most important. The other team will argue for knowledge. First, plan your arguments with your team. Try to think about what the other side will say so that you have an answer ready. Be polite but persuasive in your debate.

# Smart Solutions

What are smart ways that problems are solved?

**Comprehension**

**Skill**
Main Idea
and Details

**Strategy**
Graphic
Organizers

 # Main Idea and Details

- The topic is what a piece of writing is about.

- The main idea is the most important idea about the topic.

- Supporting details are small pieces of information. They tell about the main idea.

 ## Strategy: Graphic Organizers

A graphic organizer will help you organize information as you read. You can make a graphic organizer to show the main idea and supporting details of a piece of writing.

## Write to Read

**1.** Read "The Coldest Continent." Make a graphic organizer to show the main idea and details of the first paragraph.

**2.** Make two more graphic organizers. Show the main idea of the second paragraph and then the third paragraph.

# The Coldest Continent

Antarctica is not like any other continent. It is as far south as you can go on Earth. The South Pole is found there. Ice covers the whole land. In some places the ice is almost three miles thick! Beneath the ice are mountains and valleys.

The weather in Antarctica is harsh. It is the coldest place on Earth. The temperature does not get above freezing. It is also one of the windiest places in the world.

Not many living things are found in Antarctica. People go there to study for only a short time. Very few animals can live there. Yet many animals live on nearby islands. Seals and penguins swim in the ocean waters. They build nests on the land. Some birds spend their summers in Antarctica. But most of the continent is just ice, snow, and cold air.

**Skill** Here you can see that the topic of this passage is Antarctica, but the main idea of this paragraph is that Antarctica is covered with thick ice.

**Strategy** The last two sentences contain some supporting details.

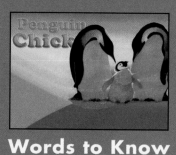

## Words to Know

hatch

pecks

snuggles

preen

flippers

frozen

cuddles

**Remember**

Try the strategy. Then, if you need more help, use your glossary or a dictionary.

# Vocabulary Strategy
## for Synonyms

**Context Clues** Sometimes when you are reading, you come across a word you don't know. The author may give you a synonym for the word. A synonym is a word that has the same or almost the same meaning as another word. Look for a word that might be a synonym. It can help you understand the meaning of the word you don't know.

**1.** Look at the words very near the word you don't know. The author may give a synonym in the same sentence.

**2.** If not, look in the sentences around the sentence with the unfamiliar word. The author may use a synonym for the word.

**3.** Try the synonym in place of the word in the sentence. Does it make sense?

As you read "Penguins Are Birds," look for synonyms to help you understand the meanings of the vocabulary words.

# Penguins Are Birds

All birds come from eggs. The mother bird lays the eggs, and then the mother bird or the father bird sits on the eggs until it is time for them to hatch. Each baby bird pecks and hits the shell of its egg with its beak until the shell breaks open. The baby bird cannot fly or get food. It needs its parents to bring it food and keep it warm. When a parent bird sits on the nest, the baby bird snuggles, or presses, into the parent's belly. The parents preen their own feathers. Then they also brush the baby bird's soft feathers. This helps keep the baby bird warm.

Penguins are birds. They have flippers instead of wings, and they swim rather than fly. But they have feathers and lay eggs just as other birds do. Baby penguins hatch from eggs, and they need their parents to give them food and warmth. Some penguins live in Antarctica, where the land and much of the water around it is frozen. Penguins don't have nests, so a penguin parent cuddles, or hugs, the egg or the chick to keep it warm.

## Words to Write

Look at the pictures on pages 158–165. Choose a picture to write about. Use words from the Words to Know list.

# Penguin Chick

by Betty Tatham
illustrated by Helen K. Davie

How do emperor penguins protect their chicks
from the extreme temperature of Antarctica?

**A** fierce wind howls. It whips snow across the ice. Here, a female emperor penguin has just laid an egg. It is the only egg she will lay this year.

Most birds build nests for their eggs. But on the ice in Antarctica, there are no twigs or leaves. There is no grass or mud. Nothing to build a nest with. Nothing but snow and ice.

The new penguin father uses his beak to scoop the egg onto his webbed feet.

He tucks it under his feather-covered skin, into a special place called a *brood patch*. The egg will be as snug and warm there as if it were in a sleeping bag.

One of the penguin parents must stay with the egg to keep it warm. But where penguins lay their eggs, there is no food for them to eat.

The penguin father is bigger and fatter than the mother. He can live longer without food. So the father penguin stays with the egg while the mother travels to the sea to find food.

The two parents sing together before the mother penguin leaves.

Along with many other penguins, the mother penguin leaves the rookery, where she laid her egg.

The mother walks or slides on her belly. This is called *tobogganing*. She uses her flippers and webbed feet to push herself forward over ice and snow.

Because it's winter in Antarctica, water near
the shore is frozen for many miles. After three days
the mother penguin comes to the end of the ice. She
dives into the water to hunt for fish, squid, and tiny
shrimplike creatures called *krill*.

**Fish**

**Squid**

**Krill**

Back at the rookery, the penguin fathers form a group called a *huddle*. They stand close together for warmth. Each keeps his own egg warm.

For two months the penguin father always keeps his egg on his feet. When he walks, he shuffles his feet so the egg doesn't roll away. He sleeps standing up. He has no food to eat, but the fat on his body keeps him alive.

Finally he feels the chick move inside the egg. The chick pecks and pecks and pecks. In about three days the egg cracks open.

The chick is wet. But soon his soft feathers, called *down,* dry and become fluffy and gray. The father still keeps the chick warm in the brood patch. Sometimes the chick pokes his head out. But while he's so little, he must stay covered. And he must stay on his father's feet. Otherwise the cold would kill him.

The father talks to the chick in his trumpet voice. The chick answers with a whistle.

The father's trumpet call echoes across the ice. The penguin mother is on her way back to the rookery, but she can't hear him. She's still too far away. If the mother doesn't come back soon with food, the chick will die.

Two days pass before the mother can hear the father penguin's call.

At last the mother arrives at the rookery. She cuddles close to the chick and trumpets to him. He whistles back. With her beak she brushes his soft gray down.

The mother swallowed many fish before she left the ocean. She brings some of this food back up from her stomach and feeds her chick. She has enough food to keep him fed for weeks. He stays on her feet and snuggles into her brood patch.

The father is very hungry, so he travels to open water. There he dives to hunt for food. Weeks later the father returns with more food for the chick.

Each day the parents preen, or brush, the chick's downy coat with their beaks. This keeps the down fluffy and keeps the chick warm.

As the chick gets bigger, he and the other chicks no longer need to stay on their parents' feet. Instead they stay together to keep warm.

This group of chicks is called a *crèche,* or a nursery. The chick now spends most of his time here. But he still rushes to his mother or father to be fed when either one comes back from the ocean.

| WINTER | | SPRING |
|---|---|---|
| *August* | *September* | *October* |

Sometimes the chick and the other young penguins dig their beaks into the ice to help them walk up a slippery hill. They toboggan down fast on their fluffy bellies.

The chick grows and grows. After five months, he has grown into a junior penguin. He is old enough to travel to the ocean.

**SUMMER**

**November**          **December**          **January**

Now he has a waterproof coat of feathers,
instead of fluffy down. He can swim in the icy cold
ocean because his feathers keep him dry and warm.

The young penguin spends most of his time in
the water. He swims, flapping his flippers as if he
were flying underwater. He uses his webbed feet to
steer wherever he wants to go.

He catches a fish with his beak and swallows
it headfirst.

Now the young penguin can catch his own food and take care of himself. In about five years he'll find a mate. Then he'll take care of his own egg until the chick can hatch.

# Reader Response

**Open for Discussion** How would you retell the information in this selection to someone who doesn't know much about emperor penguins? What are the most important parts?

1. The author is like a reporter, telling you about the emperor penguins as if you and she were there in Antarctica. Look back at page 156. Read the page aloud as if you are an on-the-scene reporter. **Think Like an Author**

2. Look back at page 163. What details support the idea that the penguin father and mother take care of the chick? **Main Idea and Details**

3. Did you create a graphic organizer to help you as you read? If so, tell how it helped you. If not, what kind of graphic organizer could you have used? Tell why. **Graphic Organizers**

4. This story is about penguin chicks. If you wrote a paragraph about barnyard chicks, which words from the Words to Know list could you use? Try it. **Vocabulary**

**Look Back and Write** Look back at page 158. What surprising thing do the parent penguins do before the mother penguin leaves? Tell why you think they do it. Use information from the selection to write the answer.

Meet author **Betty Tatham on page 417.**

# Write Now

## Summary

**Prompt**

*Penguin Chick* explains how penguins protect their eggs and their baby chicks. Think about what happens as penguin chicks hatch and grow.

Now write a summary of *Penguin Chick*.

**Writing Trait**

To help readers remember events, **organize** them in time order and in **paragraphs.**

**Time-order words help readers follow order of events.**

**Summary's main ideas are <u>organized</u> into two <u>paragraphs.</u>**

**Student Model**

Summary—Penguin Chick, pages 162–165

After the chick hatches, the father calls and waits for the mother. When she gets back, she holds the chick and brushes its down. She brings up some food she has eaten to feed the chick. It snuggles at her feet. Now the father goes to find food.

After growing a little, the chicks stay together for warmth and go to their parents for food. They use their beaks to help them walk on ice. They slide on their bellies. When they are five months old, they can travel to the ocean.

**Last sentence tells last event in time order.**

**Use the model to help you write your own summary.**

169

## Photo Essay

### Genre

- **A photo essay usually is written to inform the reader about a topic.**

- **Photo essays use photographs and text to give information.**

### Text Features

- **In this selection, arrows clearly show which photo goes with each piece of text.**

- **Some photos give a close-up view.**

### Link to Science

Use the library or the Internet to find more examples of ways that plants get sunlight and water. Report what you find to the class.

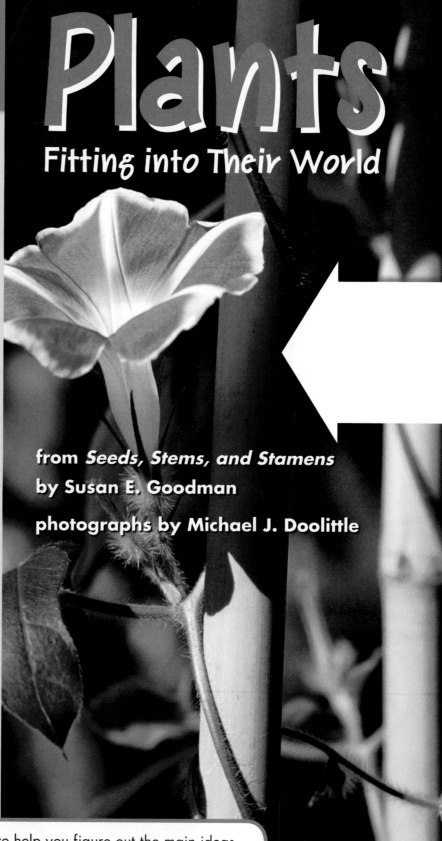

# Plants
## Fitting into Their World

from *Seeds, Stems, and Stamens*
by Susan E. Goodman

photographs by Michael J. Doolittle

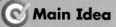 **Main Idea**  Use the heads to help you figure out the main ideas.

# Getting Sun

Almost all plants need sun to live. They use a process called *photosynthesis* to turn sunlight into food or energy. But sometimes getting enough light can be a problem. Tall plants and trees get it by growing higher than those around them. To do so, they use a lot of energy growing a strong stem or trunk. Other plants have different ways to grab their share of sunshine.

## Hitching a Ride

This **morning glory** spends its energy climbing instead. This vine uses its flexible stem to wind around strong objects and get to the light.

This **bromeliad** is a different kind of hitchhiker. It is an air plant. It grows high on a tree and uses its roots to anchor itself to the tree's trunk or upper branches.

## Leaf Placement

Many plants arrange their leaves so they can get as much sun as possible. **Mint** leaves grow in crossed pairs. That way, the leaves cast less shadow upon their neighbors.

# Getting Nutrients

Most plants get their nutrients from the soil. Some plants have evolved a different way to get their "vitamins."

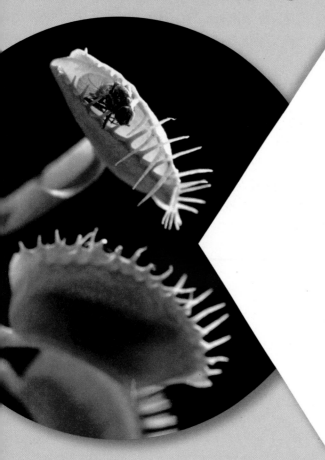

## Meat-Eaters

The leaf tips of a **Venus's-flytrap** look very tempting to an insect. They are an easy place to land. They shine with what looks to be food. Mistake! Less than a second after a bug crawls in, the trap springs shut. The bristles on the leaves point outward to keep the insect from escaping as the trap closes. The plant then uses chemicals to digest its meal. In this picture, one leaf tip has just captured a fly, while a bigger leaf tip below is in the middle of digesting another.

The inventor of sticky flypaper might have gotten the idea from a **sundew plant.** A sundew's leaves are covered with hairs. And these hairs are covered with "sundew glue." The insect that lands on a sundew is there for good. It sticks to the hairs, which fold over and trap it.

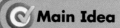 **Main Idea** | What details tell about a meat-eating Venus's-flytrap?

172

# Staying Safe

Plants can't run away from hungry insects and animals. They have developed other ways to protect themselves.

## Physical Defenses

Freeloaders like bromeliads and vines don't directly harm their host tree, but they can do damage. They soak up water and sun that the tree could have used. If too many of them pile onto a tree, they can break off its branches. This **terminalia tree** has a great defense. Every so often, it sheds its bark—and with it, most of its unwanted company.

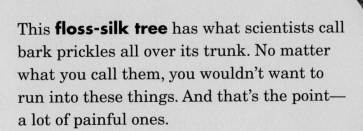

This **floss-silk tree** has what scientists call bark prickles all over its trunk. No matter what you call them, you wouldn't want to run into these things. And that's the point— a lot of painful ones.

## Reading Across Texts

Which growing thing do you think has a harder time surviving—penguin chicks or the plants in this selection?

**Writing Across Texts** Create a chart to explain why you think as you do.

 **Skill**
Character

**Strategy**
Visualize

 **Character**

- Characters are the people or animals in a story.

- Look at what a character says and does to learn what he or she is like.

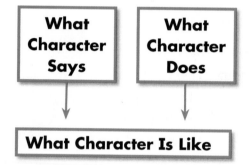

| What Character Says | What Character Does |
|---|---|

**What Character Is Like**

**Strategy: Visualize**

Active readers make pictures in their minds of what they are reading. When you read how a character acts, picture it. When you read what a character says, hear it. Visualizing will help you understand what the character is like.

## Write to Read

**1.** Read "The Grasshopper and the Ant." Make a graphic organizer like the one above. Complete it to tell what Grasshopper is like.

**2.** Use the information in your graphic organizer to write a description of Grasshopper.

# THE Grasshopper AND THE Ant

*A retelling of an Aesop fable*

On a warm summer day, Grasshopper sat in the shade and chirped. Ant walked up carrying some corn.

"Ant," said Grasshopper. "What are you doing working in the hot summer sun? Come relax in the shade with me."

"I can't," said Ant. "There is work to be done! I am storing food for the winter, and I suggest you do the same."

"Winter?" said Grasshopper. "That's a long time away. I can't be bothered about winter in the middle of summer! Are you sure you won't sit in this lovely shade with me?"

Ant just picked up the corn and went back to work.

Winter came, and the ground was cold and bare. Grasshopper had no food and lay under a bush. *I'm dying of hunger!* he thought. Nearby, the ants were eating the corn they had stored last summer. When they saw Grasshopper, they dragged some food over to him.

Grasshopper learned an important lesson. Next summer would be different.

**Strategy** Here is a good place to visualize. Picture how Grasshopper looks sitting in the shade. Hear how he talks to Ant.

**Skill** In this paragraph, notice the words that Grasshopper is using. They tell that Grasshopper is not a hard worker.

shivered

excitement

motioned

shocked

slammed

sadness

gardener

**Remember**

Try the strategy. Then, if you need more help, use your glossary or a dictionary.

# Vocabulary Strategy
## for Unfamiliar Words

**Context Clues** What do you do when you come across a word you don't know? Sometimes you can figure out what the word means by looking for context clues. Context clues are the words and sentences around the word. They can help you figure out the meaning of the word.

**1.** Read the words and sentences around the word you don't know. Sometimes the author tells you what the word means.

**2.** If not, use the words and sentences to predict a meaning for the word.

**3.** Try that meaning in the sentence. Does it make sense?

As you read "A Gardening Adventure," use context clues to help you understand the meanings of the vocabulary words.

# A Gardening Adventure

Dear Anna,

This year I decided to plant a flower garden in the backyard. I was in a hurry to get started, so I planted the seeds in late March. It was still cold out, and I shivered as I dug the holes. However, I figured spring would be here soon. A week later, tiny green shoots were poking up out of the ground. Each morning, I rushed outside with great excitement to see how much they had grown.

Then yesterday morning when I came into the kitchen, my mother motioned to me to come to the window.

I was shocked to see that everything outside was coated with ice—including my plants! They looked as if someone had slammed a heavy weight down on them. I felt such sadness.

Later, the sun came out, and the ice began to melt. When I looked at my plants again, they were standing up straight and green. I can't wait for them to flower, but I've learned my lesson. Next year, this gardener will wait until late April to start her garden!

Love,
Cecilia

## Words to Write

Look at this picture. Write about what has happened to the flower. Use words from the Words to Know list.

# A Day's Work

by Eve Bunting
illustrated by Ronald Himler

**Genre**

**Realistic fiction** is a story that could really happen.
Has anything like this happened to you?

Francisco wants very much to help his grandfather.
What could possibly go wrong?

Francisco stood in the parking lot with his
grandfather and the other men. It was the first time
he'd been there.

A truck cruised along, slowed.

The driver held up three fingers. "Bricklaying.
I need three men," he called.

Five men jumped in the back.

"Only three," the driver said, and two had to
get out.

The workers left in the parking lot grumbled and
shuffled around.

Francisco's grandfather shivered. *"Hace frío,"*
he said.

"It is cold because it is still early. It will be hot later, you will see," Francisco said in Spanish.

"Why did you bring a kid?" one of the men asked. "No one will hire you with a kid. He belongs in school."

"It's Saturday," Francisco said. "My *abuelo,* my grandfather, does not speak English yet. He came to California only two days ago to live with my mother and me."

Francisco swallowed. "We have been alone—since my father died. I am going to help my *abuelo* get work."

He took his grandfather's cold, rough hand and smiled up at him. Abuelo was tall and skinny as an old tree. Already Francisco loved him. When there was money to spare they'd get him a jacket like Francisco's with sleeves long enough to cover his hands. And an L.A. Lakers cap like Francisco's too.

A van was coming. BENJAMIN'S GARDENING was printed on the side.

Francisco let go of his grandfather's hand. He darted through the swarm of men and was right in front of the van when it stopped.

"One man," the driver said. "For gardening." He was young, with a thick, black mustache. And he was wearing an L.A. Lakers cap, like Francisco's. Maybe cleaner. It must be an omen, Francisco thought.

"Take us, Mr. Benjamin. *Us.*" Francisco pointed back at his grandfather. He tilted his own cap over his eyes. "Look! We love the Lakers, too. And my grandfather is a fine gardener, though he doesn't know English yet. The gardens are the same, right? Mexican and American?"

Francisco waved urgently for his grandfather to come. "Also, you will get two for one," he said. "I don't charge for my work."

The man grinned. "OK. I'm convinced. But I'm not Mr. Benjamin. Call me Ben."

He motioned to Francisco. "You and your grandfather jump in back. Sixty dollars for the day."

Francisco nodded. His breath was coming fast. That much for a day's work? Mama would be so happy. Her job didn't pay much. There'd be extra food tonight, maybe *chorizos.*

He pulled open the back door, threw in the bag of lunch Mama had packed, and hurried his grandfather into the van ahead of him.

A big, tough guy tried to get in too. Francisco pushed him back. *He* was tough. He was a worker.

"It is gardening," he told Abuelo as the van pulled away.

"But I do not know gardening. I am a carpenter. I have always lived in the city."

"It is easy." Francisco waved through the window at the passing cars. "Flowers, roses, things like that." He raised his cap to a lady in a car. "*Señora,*" he said politely, though she couldn't hear.

The van turned off the freeway onto a winding road and stopped. A sloping bank led up to the backyards of new houses. Some were not yet finished. Workers climbed high on rooftops, and there was the good smell of tar.

The high bank was dotted with pretty white flowers and overgrown with coarse green spikes. Six big black trash cans waited below.

They all got out of the van but Ben left the motor running.

"I need you to weed this bank," he told Abuelo. "Be sure to get the roots." He pointed to the cans. "Dump them here."

"Good. Fine." It was Francisco who answered.

"I have another job to go to," Ben said. "I'll pick you up at three. It will be hot. Your grandfather will need a hat." He took a straw one from the van.

"*Gracias,*" Abuelo said.

"See you guys then. Work hard. Have a nice day."

"What did he say?" Abuelo asked as the van drove off.

"He said to have a nice day. It is what everyone says up here."

"Your English is very good, my grandson," Abuelo said.

Francisco nodded and smiled. He climbed the bank and hung his jacket on a railing. "Now," he said, "I will show you." He pulled up one of the spiky clumps and shook the dirt from its roots. "These are weeds. Do not touch the flowers."

185

His grandfather smiled. *"Bueno."* Francisco could see his strong white teeth all the way to the back.

They worked through the morning.

A little poodle barked at them through the railings above. "Yap, yap, yap."

An orange cat prowled the bank.

There was a pool in one of the new backyards. Francisco heard splashing and voices. The water sounds made him hotter. His shoulders and arms hurt. He thought about how proud Mama would be tonight.

"Sixty dollars?" she'd say, and she'd hug Francisco and Abuelo. "It is a fortune."

At lunchtime he and Abuelo ate the tortillas and tomatoes and drank the bottle of water she had packed.

In another hour they were finished.

The bank looked so nice with just the brown dirt and the pretty flowers.

*"Muy bonito,"* Abuelo said.

And Francisco said, "Yes, beautiful!"

He and his grandfather shook hands.

Francisco thought he had never felt so good. He'd helped his grandfather, and he had worked himself.

They sat on the curb to wait for the van, and when it came they stood and brushed the loose dirt from their clothes.

Ben got out and stared up at the bank. "Holy Toledo!" he said.

"You didn't think we could do such a good job?" Francisco wanted to laugh, Ben seemed so shocked.

Francisco gave a little jump and pretended to slam dunk a ball. "Like the Lakers. We work hard."

"I can't believe it!" Ben whispered. "You . . . you took out all the plants and left the weeds."

Francisco stepped closer to Abuelo. "But the flowers . . . ," he began.

Ben pointed. "Those flowers are chickweed. Chickweed! You took out my young ice plants!" He yanked off his Lakers cap and slammed it against the van.

"What is it? Did we do something wrong?" Abuelo
whispered in Spanish to Francisco.

Ben's mustache quivered with anger. "I thought
you said your grandfather was a fine gardener. He
doesn't even know a *chickweed?*"

Abuelo looked from one of them to the other. "Tell
me what is happening, Francisco," he said.

"We left the weeds. We took out the plants,"
Francisco said softly in Spanish. It was hard to look at
his grandfather as he spoke.

"He thought we knew about gardening," Abuelo
said. His Spanish was fast and angry. "You lied to him.
Isn't that so?"

"We needed a day's work . . . ."

"We do not lie for work."

Now there was more sadness than anger in Abuelo's voice. "Ah, my grandson." He put a hand on Francisco's shoulder. "Ask him what we can do. Tell him we will come back tomorrow, if he agrees. We will pull out the weeds and put the good plants back."

Francisco felt his heart go weak. "But . . . but Abuelo, that will be twice the work. And tomorrow is Sunday. There is a Lakers game on TV. And there is also church." He hoped the word *church* would perhaps change his grandfather's thinking.

"We will miss them both, then," his grandfather said. "It is the price of the lie. Tell the gentleman what I said, and ask him if the plants will live."

Ben said they would. "The roots are still there. If they're replanted early, they'll be all right."

He rubbed his eyes. "This is partly my fault. I should have stayed to get you started. But tell your grandfather I appreciate his offer, and I'll bring you back in the morning."

The three of them got in the van.

Francisco sat by the window in huddled silence. He didn't wave to passing cars. He didn't raise his cap. He'd helped his grandfather find work. But in the end the lie had spoiled the day. His throat burned with tears.

The parking lot was empty. The trash can overflowed
with used paper cups and sandwich wrappings.

Ben let them out.

"Look," he said. "If you need money I'll give you
half now." He began to pull his wallet from his pocket
but Abuelo held up his hand.

"Tell him we take the pay tomorrow, when we finish."

Francisco's grandfather and Ben looked at each other and words seemed to pass between them, though there were no words. Ben slid his wallet back into his pocket.

Francisco sighed. The lie had taken the *chorizos,* too.

"Tomorrow then. Six A.M.," Ben said. "And tell your grandfather I can always use a good man—for more than just one day's work."

Francisco gave a hop of excitement. More than just a day's work!

Ben was still speaking. "The important things your grandfather knows already. And I can teach him gardening."

Francisco nodded. He understood. He would tell his grandfather, and he would tell him something else. He, Francisco, had begun to learn the important things, too.

Francisco took his grandfather's cold, rough hand in his. "Let's go home, Abuelo," he said.

# Reader Response

**Open for Discussion**  What do you think happened to Francisco and his grandfather the next day and the day after that and the day after that?

**1.** The author, Eve Bunting, has written more than a hundred stories. How do you think she got the idea for *A Day's Work*?  **Think Like an Author**

**2.** What can you say about Francisco? What was he like? What words would you use to describe him?  **Character**

**3.** What picture did you have in your mind of Francisco and his grandfather working in the hot sun? How did that help you as you read?  **Visualize**

**4.** Imagine how Francisco felt at the end of the story. Write a journal entry as Francisco, use words from the Words to Know list.  **Vocabulary**

**Look Back and Write**  On page 191 Ben says, "The important things your grandfather knows already." Explain what Ben means when he says that. Use details from the story.

**Meet author Eve Bunting on page 408.**

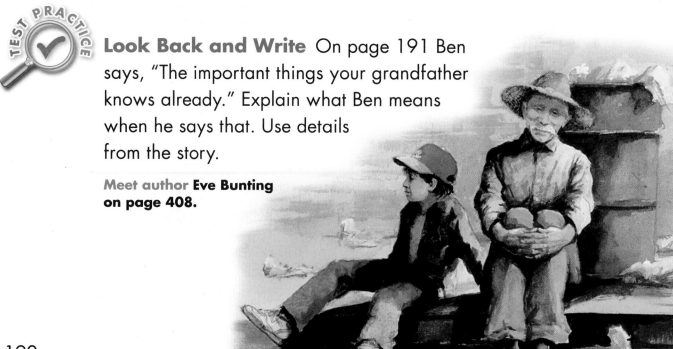

192

# Write Now

## Rules

### Prompt

*A Day's Work* describes one rule for living and getting along with others.
Think about rules for getting along with family members, friends, or neighbors.
Now write the rules as commands.

**Writing Trait**

Writing rules calls for using one kind of **sentence—** commands.

**Student Model**

**Rules are written in a numbered list.**

**Rules may include specific details.**

### Rules for Living with Your Little Sister

1. Do nice things, such as read her a story.
2. Teach her something, such as how to tie her shoes.
3. Let her play with your toys sometimes.
4. Encourage her instead of teasing her.
5. Be patient even when it seems like she is bothering you.
6. Be pleasant to her when your friends come over.
7. Be friendly when she is playing with other kids.

**Each rule is the same kind of <u>sentence</u>— a command.**

**Use the model to help you write your own rules.**

## E-Mail

### Genre

- The letter *e* in *e-mail* stands for *electronic*. An e-mail is a message sent by computer over the Internet from one user to another.

- E-mail lets you communicate with people all over the world.

### Text Features

- The *To:* box shows to whom a message is going.

- The message itself looks like the body of a letter.

### Link to Science

Find examples of weeds in your neighborhood. Bring them to class and use a resource to label them.

# What Is a Weed?

Francisco and his *abuelo* got in trouble because they pulled up the wrong plants. "Tomorrow," Francisco told himself, "I will be smarter! I will know a weed from a flower!" That night, Francisco went to a computer and used e-mail to help him learn about plants.

For more practice

**Take It to the Net**

PearsonSuccessNet.com

At a gardening Web site, Francisco found a link labeled *Contact Us,* so he wrote an e-mail.

File   Edit   View   Favorites   Tools   Help

http://www.url.here

# Gardening & Horticulture

Send   Attach   Address

To:   email address here

Cc:

Subject:   Plant or Weed?

The e-mail address of the person you are writing to goes here.

Sometimes, you do not know to whom you are addressing your e-mail. In that case, use Dear Sir or Madam.

Dear Sir or Madam:

I got in trouble today. I had a job to weed a garden, but I pulled out all the flowers and left all the weeds! Help me! How can I tell the difference? Thank you.

Francisco

**Main Idea**   What's the main idea of this message?

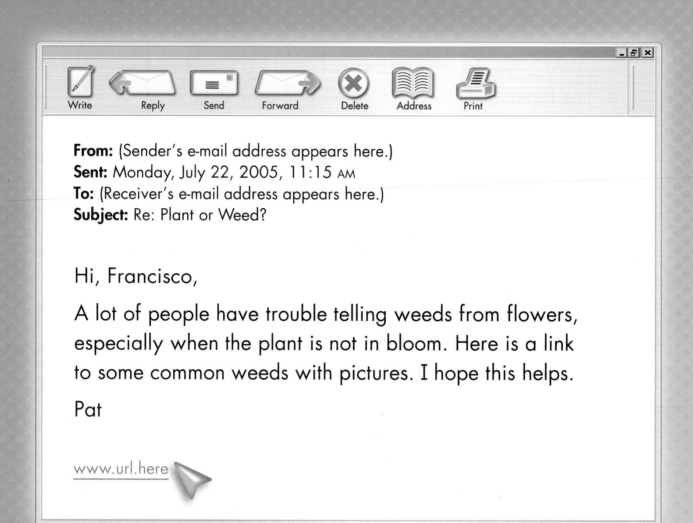

**From:** (Sender's e-mail address appears here.)
**Sent:** Monday, July 22, 2005, 11:15 AM
**To:** (Receiver's e-mail address appears here.)
**Subject:** Re: Plant or Weed?

Hi, Francisco,

A lot of people have trouble telling weeds from flowers, especially when the plant is not in bloom. Here is a link to some common weeds with pictures. I hope this helps.

Pat

www.url.here

Francisco was really excited. He clicked on the link and found this information.

Edit    View    Favorites    Tools    Help

http://www.url.here

# *Common Weeds*

## Canada Thistle

Canada thistle is a creeping plant that returns every year. The foliage is spiny.

## Dandelion

The dandelion returns every year. It has a long root. Its yellow flowers can bloom anytime between March and November.

### Purslane

Purslane is a summer weed. It has thick leaves and small yellow flowers. The plant is low-growing. It is easily pulled when the soil is wet.

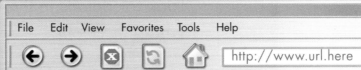

---

### Reading Across Texts

Now that Francisco has this information, what advice would you give him about his next job as a gardener?

**Writing Across Texts** Write an e-mail to Francisco giving him your advice.

---

 **Visualize**  Try to visualize the weeds as you read about them.

**Comprehension**

**Skill**
Main Idea

**Strategy**
Monitor
and Fix Up

# Main Idea

- When you read a story, ask yourself, "What is this story all about?"

- Details are small pieces of information. Look for details in the story that help tell what it is about.

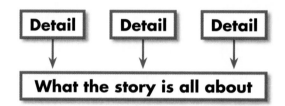

| Detail | Detail | Detail |
|--------|--------|--------|

**What the story is all about**

## Strategy: Monitor and Fix Up

Good readers stop when they are confused and figure out what's wrong. Summing up can help. As you read, ask yourself, "What are the important details in this story so far?" That will help you make sure you understand what is happening. It will also help you tell what the story is all about.

## Write to Read

1. Read "The Stamp Collector." Make a chart like the one above. Write details and then a statement of what the story is about.

2. Use your chart to write a short summary of the story "The Stamp Collector."

# The Stamp Collector

Carlos grabbed the envelope from Rosa's hand.

"Don't tell me," said Rosa. "You want the stamp. Is there anything more boring than collecting stamps? You put them in a book and then what? You can't even play with them."

"What do *you* know?" replied Carlos. "You collect beads."

"I don't collect them. I make beautiful bead jewelry," Rosa said. "People can wear my jewelry. What good is a book of stamps?"

That evening Carlos cut a stamp from a postcard he had bought at a yard sale. It was a 30¢ stamp with a picture of George Washington on it. He looked it up in a stamp catalog. Carlos carefully matched his stamp with the picture in the catalog. Suddenly he began jumping around. "One of my stamps is worth between 100 and 300 dollars!" Carlos exclaimed.

"Let me see that!" Rosa demanded.

"No," Carlos laughed. "You said looking at stamps is boring."

**Strategy** If you're having trouble, this would be a good place to stop and do something about it. Sum up the story so far. That might help.

**Skill** You've read several details so far. What would you say is the main idea of this story?

199

enormous

scattered

strain

realize

collection

shiny

# Vocabulary Strategy
## for Unfamiliar Words

**Dictionary** You can always use a dictionary to find out the meaning of a word you don't know. A dictionary tells you the word's meaning and how to say the word. The words in a dictionary are listed in alphabetical order.

**1.** Look at the first letter in the word and turn in the dictionary to the section for that letter.

**2.** Use the guide words at the top of each page and what you know about the alphabet to help you find the word.

**3.** Read the definitions. If the word has more than one meaning, decide which meaning you think fits in the sentence.

**4.** Try that meaning in the sentence to see if it makes sense.

Read "Get Organized." Use a dictionary to find out the meanings of the vocabulary words.

# Get Organized

Are there enormous piles of stuff in your room? Are your things scattered everywhere? Is your closet clutter putting a strain on the door? Then it's time to take action!

First, realize that this will take time and work. Look at each thing. Ask yourself, "Do I use this? Will I ever use this?" This information will help you decide what to get rid of and what to keep. Take the things you are getting rid of. Put them in large trash bags. Are they in good shape? Give them away to a charity. If not, throw them out.

Next, take the things you are keeping. Put them into groups. Put each group together in one place. Put all the books on a shelf or table. Hang the clothes in the closet or put them in drawers. Do you have a collection of objects, such as rocks, postcards, or stamps? Display them together on a shelf, table, or wall.

Now vacuum and dust your room. Congratulations! You have a shiny, clean, and well-organized room.

## Words to Write

What do you collect? Write about your collection. Tell why you like to collect. Use as many words from the Words to Know list as you can.

**Genre** A **fantasy** includes make-believe events. Look for situations that could not happen.

# Prudy's Problem

## and How She Solved It

by Carey Armstrong-Ellis

What happens when Prudy's problem gets out of control?

Prudy seemed like a normal little girl. She had a sister. She had a dog. She had two white mice. She had a mom and a dad and her own room at home.

Yes, Prudy seemed normal.

But Prudy collected things.

Now most kids collect something. Prudy's friend Egbert collected butterflies. So did Prudy.

Belinda had a stamp collection. So did Prudy.

Harold collected tin foil and made it into a big ball. So did Prudy.

All her friends had collections. And so did Prudy— but Prudy collected *everything*.

She saved rocks, feathers, leaves, twigs, dead bugs, and old flowers. She kept a box full of interesting fungi in the bottom drawer of her dresser. She saved every picture she had ever drawn and every valentine she had ever gotten. She saved pretty paper napkins from parties and kept them in her desk drawer. She had six hundred and fourteen stuffed animals in different unnatural colors.

205

She had collections of ribbons, shoelaces, souvenir postcards, flowered fabric scraps, pencils with fancy ends, pink scarves with orange polka dots, old calendars, salt and pepper shakers with faces, dried-out erasers, plastic lizards, pointy sunglasses, china animals, heart-shaped candy boxes with the paper candy cups still inside, tufts of hair from different breeds of dogs . . . .

She just could not throw anything away.

It drove her dad to distraction.
He was a very tidy person who did not
like clutter. He started saying unpleasant
things as he tried to mow the lawn.

"Prudy, you have a problem," he said.

"What do you mean?" she asked, baffled.

"You just have too much stuff. Why don't
we haul it all to the dump?" he suggested
hopefully.

"I don't have too much stuff, Dad,"
Prudy said.

It even got to be too much for her mom, who did not mind clutter but could no longer navigate the living room.

"Maybe you could take all this to the thrift shop," she said. "Surely someone could use this old mushroom . . . ."

"I *like* that mushroom," Prudy said.

"Prudy, you have to face your problem," said her mother.

"I do not have a problem," said Prudy.

Prudy's little sister started putting together collections of her own.

"Uh-oh," said Egbert, eyeing Evie's little piles of pine twigs and used toothbrushes. "Prudy, how about if you packed everything all up and stuffed it into a rocket and sent it to Neptune?"

"Yeah, that would solve your problem!" agreed Harold and Belinda.

*"There is no problem!"* shouted Prudy.

But Prudy herself found that she could barely get to her desk to feed her mice.

# SALSA GARDEN

David saw the sign his father put on the garden fence. It said Salsa Garden.

"Salsa?" David read aloud. "Can you grow salsa?"

Dad replied, "Just watch and see what comes up."

Each time David helped by watering and pulling weeds, he looked at the green plants. They all looked different. Not one looked like salsa.

Finally, harvest time came. First, Dad dug in the ground and pulled out round white things that looked a lot like onions. Then, he pulled off pods hanging from a plant. They looked a lot like hot peppers. Next, he cut a green leafy plant that smelled spicy. Finally, Dad pulled round, red balls from a fat vine. They sure looked a lot like tomatoes.

"Where's the salsa, Dad?" David asked as he followed his father to the kitchen.

Dad washed and cut everything up. He dumped his harvest into a machine with a sharp blade and turned it on. When he opened the lid, it was full of salsa!

**Strategy** Make a prediction here. What do you think this story will be about? Why would an author write a story with this title? Maybe it will tell about making salsa.

**Skill** Now we can determine the author's purpose. What do you think? Perhaps he wanted to inform us that good salsa needs good garden-grown vegetables.

225

lazy

bottom

crops

clever

cheated

partners

wealth

**Remember**

Try the strategy. Then, if you need more help, use your glossary or a dictionary.

# Vocabulary Strategy
## for Antonyms

**Context Clues** Sometimes when you are reading, you come across a word you don't know. The author may give you an antonym for the word. An antonym is a word that means the opposite of a word. For example, *empty* is the opposite of *full.* Look for a word that might be an antonym. It can help you understand the meaning of a word you don't know.

**1.** Look at the words around the word you don't know. The author may have used an antonym.

**2.** Look for words that seem to have opposite meanings. Think about the word you know.

**3.** Use that word to help you figure out the meaning of its antonym.

As you read "Farming," look for antonyms to help you understand the meanings of the vocabulary words.

# Farming

Farming is not an occupation for lazy people. Farmers are always busy. In the spring they till, or turn up, the soil to prepare it for planting. Then they dig holes, put the seeds in the bottom of each hole, and cover them with soil. In the summer, farmers water and weed the growing crops. In the fall, it is time for harvesting. Then they cut or dig up the crops in the fields. In some countries, farmers use machines to do these things. In many countries, however, farmers still do many jobs by hand.

The weather can make any farmer look clever or foolish. Too much rain and the crops wash away; not enough rain and the crops die. The weather has often cheated farmers and ruined their crops. So farmers must be partners with the weather.

Most farmers do not make a lot of money. So why do they farm? Some farm to get the food they need. Many choose to be farmers because to them wealth is not as important as working with the land.

## Words to Write

Would you like to be a farmer? Why or why not? Write about your ideas. Use words from the Words to Know list.

**Genre**

An **animal fantasy** is a story with animal characters that behave like people. Look for ways that Bear and Hare act like people.

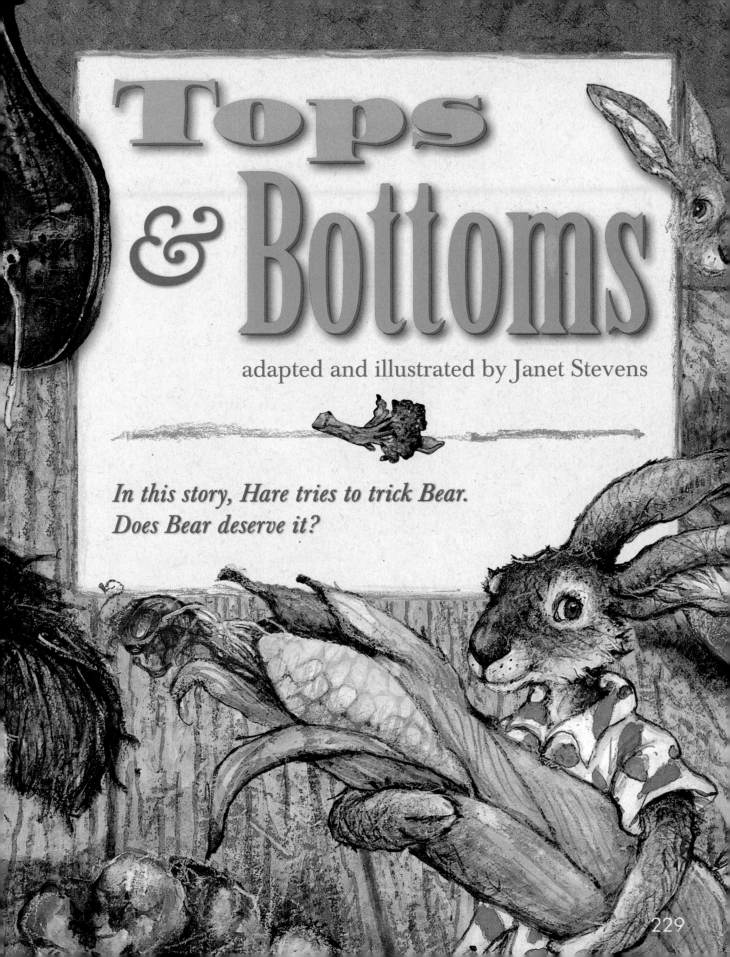

# Tops & Bottoms

adapted and illustrated by Janet Stevens

*In this story, Hare tries to trick Bear.*
*Does Bear deserve it?*

nce upon a time there lived a very lazy bear who had lots of money and lots of land. His father had been a hard worker and a smart business bear, and he had given all of his wealth to his son.

But all Bear wanted to do was sleep.

Not far down the road lived a hare. Although Hare was clever, he sometimes got into trouble. He had once owned land, too, but now he had nothing. He had lost a risky bet with a tortoise and had sold all of his land to Bear to pay off the debt.

Hare and his family were in very bad shape.

"The children are so hungry, Father Hare! We must think of something!" Mrs. Hare cried one day. So Hare and Mrs. Hare put their heads together and cooked up a plan.

The next day Hare hopped down the road to Bear's house. Bear, of course, was asleep.

"Hello, Bear, wake up! It's your neighbor, Hare, and I have an idea!"

Bear opened one eye and grunted.

"We can be business partners!" Hare said. "All we need is this field right here in front of your house. I'll do the hard work of planting and harvesting, and we can split the profit right down the middle. Yes, sir, Bear, we're in this together. I'll work and you sleep."

"Huh?" said Bear.

"So, what will it be, Bear?" asked Hare. "The top half or the bottom half? It's up to you–tops or bottoms."

"Uh, let's see," Bear said with a yawn.
"I'll take the top half, Hare. Right–tops."
Hare smiled. "It's a done deal, Bear."
So Bear went back to sleep, and Hare
and his family went to work. Hare planted,
Mrs. Hare watered, and everyone weeded.

Bear slept as the crops grew.

When it was time for the harvest, Hare called out, "Wake up, Bear! You get the tops and I get the bottoms."

Hare and his family dug up the carrots,
the radishes, and the beets. Hare plucked off
all the tops, tossed them into a pile for Bear,
and put the bottoms aside for himself.

Bear stared at his pile. "But, Hare, all the best parts are in your half!"

"You chose the tops, Bear," Hare said.

"Now, Hare, you've tricked me. You plant this field again—and this season I want the bottoms!"

Hare agreed. "It's a done deal, Bear."

So Bear went back to sleep, and Hare and his family went to work. They planted, watered, and weeded.

Bear slept as the crops grew.

When it was time for the harvest, Hare called out, "Wake up, Bear! You get the bottoms and I get the tops."

Hare and his family gathered up the lettuce, the broccoli, and the celery. Hare pulled off the bottoms for Bear and put the tops in his own pile.

Bear looked at his pile and scowled. "Hare, you have cheated me again."

"But, Bear," Hare said, "you wanted the bottoms this time."

Bear growled, "You plant this field again, Hare. You've tricked me twice, and you owe me one season of both tops and bottoms!"

"You're right, poor old Bear," sighed Hare. "It's only fair that you get both tops and bottoms this time. It's a done deal, Bear."

So Bear went back to sleep, and Hare and his family went to work. They planted, watered, and weeded, then watered and weeded some more.

Bear slept as the crops grew.

When it was time for the harvest, Hare called out, "Wake up, Bear! This time you get the tops and the bottoms!"

There in front of Bear's house lay a high field of corn. Hare and his family yanked up every cornstalk. Hare tugged off the roots at the bottom and the tassels at the top and put them in a pile for Bear. Then he carefully collected the ears of corn in the middle and placed them in his own pile.

242

Bear rubbed his eyes and watched.

"See, Bear? You get the tops and the bottoms. I get the middles. Yes, sir, Bear. It's a done deal!"

By now Bear was wide awake. "That's it, Hare!" he hollered. "From now on I'll plant my own crops and take the tops, bottoms, and middles!"

Hare and his family scooped up the corn and hopped down the road toward home.

243

Bear never again slept through a season
of planting and harvesting. Hare bought back
his land with the profit from the crops, and
he and Mrs. Hare opened a vegetable stand.

And although Hare and Bear learned to live happily as neighbors, they never became business partners again!

# Reader Response

**Open for Discussion** Bear and Hare—what a pair! Get together with a partner and act out the story to retell it. Act out the story twice, until it's a done deal!

1.  Janet Stevens must have had fun making the pictures. Pretend you can step into one of the pictures. Look around. Tell everything you see, smell, and hear.
    **Think Like an Author**

2.  Why do you think the author chose to use the hare as the main character in this story? **Author's Purpose**

3.  Did you predict that Bear would get nothing after the first harvest? How did that prediction help you with your next prediction? **Predict**

4.  Bear and Hare are very different from each other. Make a Venn diagram to show how they are alike and different. Label the circles Bear and Hare. Label the middle section Both. Use words from the Words to Know list and from the story to fill in your diagram. **Vocabulary**

**Look Back and Write** Bear and Hare both had problems. Were their problems solved at the end of the story? How? Look back to the end of the selection. Use details from the selection to write your answer.

**Meet author and illustrator
Janet Stevens on page 415.**

# Write Now

## Feature Story

**Prompt**

In *Tops and Bottoms*, a character uses his creativity to get ahead.

Think about an event that happened because of one or more creative people.

Now write a feature story about the event and the person.

**Writing Trait**

A strong, lively **voice** will both inform and entertain your readers.

**Student Model**

**Question at beginning engages readers.**

Are you an artist or art lover? Then meet nine-year-old Clark Peterson. Clark and his friends are artists. He had a brilliant idea—open an art gallery in a vacant shop. But who would pay the rent? Clark contacted artists who wanted to display their work. Twenty people chipped in rent money. When the gallery opened, many people came to view and buy the artwork. The artists use some of the money to keep the gallery going. Thanks to Clark Peterson, Milltown's artists and art lovers are happy.

**Details and word choice contribute to lively, interested voice.**

**Last sentence echoes first sentence to emphasize main idea.**

**Use the model to help you write your own feature story.**

## Fable

### Genre

- Animals are often the main characters in a fable.
- The author tells a very brief story that clearly points to a moral or a lesson.
- The moral is usually stated at the end of the story, highlighting its importance.

### Link to Reading

Find other fables in the library. Report other morals or lessons you find to your class.

# The Hare and the Tortoise

by Aesop
illustrated by Michael Hague

One day a quick-footed Hare was making fun of a slow-moving Tortoise. Much to the Hare's surprise, the Tortoise began to laugh. "I challenge you to a race," said the Tortoise, "and I bet that I will win."

"Very well," said the Hare, "I will dance rings around you all the way."

It was soon agreed that the Fox would set the course and be the judge. The race began and the Hare ran so quickly that he soon left the Tortoise far behind. Once he reached the middle of the course, the Hare decided to take a nap.

While the Hare slept, the Tortoise plodded on and on, straight toward the finish line. When the Hare awoke from his nap, he was surprised that the Tortoise was nowhere in sight. Racing to the finish line as fast as he could, the Hare was shocked to find the Tortoise waiting for him with a smile on his face.

*Slow and steady wins the race.*

**Reading Across Texts**

Who were the winner and the loser in this story and in *Tops and Bottoms*? Why did the loser lose each time?

**Writing Across Texts** Write a short paragraph comparing the losers.

**Author's Purpose** What lesson is the author trying to teach?

249

 # Draw Conclusions

Skill

- A conclusion is a decision you reach after you think about details and facts.

- As you read, think about the details and facts and use what you already know to draw conclusions about characters and the things that happen.

$$\text{Fact or Detail} + \text{What You Already Know} = \text{Conclusion}$$

 ## Strategy: Ask Questions

Strategy

Active readers ask themselves questions as they read. As you read, ask why certain things happen or why characters act as they do. The answers may not be given in a sentence, but you may be able to draw conclusions about them.

# Write to Read

1. Read "How to Build an Adobe House." Make a graphic organizer like the one above. Draw a conclusion about laying adobe out in the sun.

2. Use the information in "How to Build an Adobe House" and what you know to write a conclusion about the kind of weather needed to make adobe.

# How to Build an Adobe House

Adobe is a kind of brick. Adobe bricks have been used to build desert houses for many years. You can see adobe houses in the desert Southwest of our country.

To build a house of adobe, you need clay. Add water and dirt to the clay. Let it stand for a day or two. It will become soft. Then, mix in a little straw to make a paste. This will hold the brick together. Next, put the paste into molds. Each mold is made of pieces of wood put together in the shape of a brick. Then leave the bricks in the sun for about two weeks.

Once you have made the bricks, you can build your house. Add a roof, and your house is done! You will be warm in the winter and cool in the summer.

**Strategy** This is a good place to ask a question, such as, *"Why would I leave the bricks in the sun?"*

**Skill** Then you can use the details you have just read and what you already know about the sun to draw the conclusion that the sun will harden the bricks.

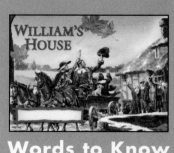

**Words to Know**

clearing

pegs

steep

cellar

barrels

spoil

**Remember**

Try the strategy. Then, if you need more help, use your glossary or a dictionary.

# Vocabulary Strategy
## for Unfamiliar Words

**Context Clues** Sometimes when you are reading, you come across a word you don't know. How can you figure out what the word means? Look for context clues. Context clues are the words and sentences around the word. They can help you figure out the meaning of the word.

**1.** Read the words and sentences around the word you don't know. Sometimes the author tells you what the word means.

**2.** If not, use the words and sentences to predict a meaning for the word.

**3.** Try that meaning in the sentence. Does it make sense?

As you read "Like the Good Old Days," use context clues to help you understand the meanings of the vocabulary words.

# Like the Good Old Days

Look at the photograph. These people are pretending to be colonists in the 1600s. They are called *reenactors*. They want to do things the way the colonists did. They built a house like one the colonists built.

First, the reenactors cut down trees to make a clearing, or open space. They used whole logs to make the frame of the house, and they split logs into planks, or boards, to make the walls. They carved pegs out of wood and used the pegs, instead of nails, to hold the logs and planks together. Finally, they put a very steep roof on the house so that the snow would slide off.

Behind the house the reenactors dug a cellar, or underground room. They put food into barrels and stored the barrels in the cool, dry cellar so that the food wouldn't spoil. This was one way the colonists kept their food fresh. They also salted their meat and dried their vegetables.

## Words to Write

Look at the picture. Write about what you think it would be like to live in a colonial house. Use words from the Words to Know list.

253

# WILLIAM'S HOUSE

by Ginger Howard

illustrated by Larry Day

What is special about William's house?

## New England, 1637

William knew just the kind of house he wanted. It would be like the house he grew up in, his father's house, in England.

William cleared an area 20 feet square. He used the felled trees for the upright posts. The saplings were used for the fence. Then he went to the woods and cut rafters to hold the thatch roof. He split planks for clapboards. And he fashioned wood pegs to hold everything in place.

William's wife, Elizabeth, wanted a window, but William had no glass. He scraped a piece of animal horn until it was translucent. Then he made a wide slit in the clapboards and covered the opening with the horn.

William used clay and stones from the creek bed to build a small fireplace in one corner of the room. He placed two pegs on the wall, one for his extra shirt, and one for his wife's apron. Then he made a board table with the side of a packing crate. And finally, he stuffed bags with corn husks for beds.

When all was done, William and Elizabeth and
their two sons sat at the board. They dipped their
fingers into trenchers of pudding and bread. A noggin
of cider was passed from hand to hand. After supper,
they folded their long napkins and put them in
the chest.

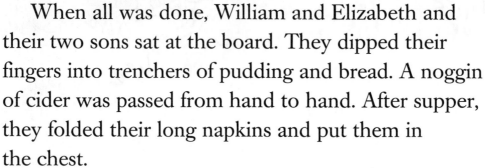

As soon as it was dark, William covered the glowing
embers with ashes. William and his wife climbed into
bed, and the boys climbed onto the table to sleep.
William smiled. He thought of the new house, and
it was just like the one he grew up in, his father's
house, in England.

The days grew longer, and soon it was summer.

"It is hotter here than at home in England,"
said William.

The barrels of pork began to spoil, and the root vegetables began to sprout.

"Something must be done," said his wife, "or we'll have no food!"

So William dug a hole deep in the cool earth behind the house. He moved the barrels and the vegetables into the new cellar.

In August, the winds started to blow.

"It is windier here than at home in England," said William.

A strong gust blew a tree down near the house.

"Something must be done," said his wife, "or we'll be crushed!"

So William cut away the trees and left a large clearing all around the house.

By mid–October, the reds and oranges of autumn had turned to browns.

"It is drier here than at home in England," said William.

The sparks from the chimney landed on the dry thatch, and the roof began to smolder.

"Something must be done," said his wife, "or the house will burn!"

So William split shingles of cedar and replaced the thatch on the roof.

By late November, the days were short and gray.

"There is more snow here than at home in England," said William.

The snow piled higher and higher on the roof until the rafters sagged with the weight.

"Something must be done," said his wife, "or the roof will cave in!"

So William cleared the snow and removed the shingles. He built a new roof with a very steep pitch and replaced the shingles.

In January, the days were the bleakest of all.

"It is colder here than at home in England," said William.

The boys could not move their toes when they woke in the morning, and the dog could not wag his tail.

"Something must be done," said his wife, "or we'll freeze in our sleep!"

So William built a new fireplace, wider and taller, in the center of the wall.

One day, the sun was strong enough to melt the frozen crust on the newly formed buds. Spring had arrived. And with it, a ship from England sailed into the harbor.

Familiar voices calling through the trees brought a quick halt to the family's work. William's face lit up as he, Elizabeth, and the boys all ran to greet Cousin Samuel and his wife, Constance. There were hugs and laughs and bursts of news and even more hugs.

And then, Cousin Samuel turned toward the clearing. "What kind of house is this?" he asked.

William turned also and took a long look at the house. The window was a piece of animal horn. The food was in a cellar. The house stood in a clearing. The roof was very steep and made of shingles. The fireplace was large and in the center of the wall. The house did not look like his father's house in England.

William looked at his wife.

Then he turned to his cousin and answered, "This is our new home. Welcome!"

They all went inside. The adults sat above the salt and the children stood below. They shared trenchers of succotash stew and passed around a noggin of cider.

# Reader Response

**Open for Discussion** William's house isn't quite the way he planned it. Tell why.

1. This story happened more than 300 years ago. Still, some readers may feel as if they know William, his family, and his house. How have the author and the artist helped give that feeling? **Think Like an Author**

2. Knowing the changes that William made to his new house, what could you say about houses built in the new land? **Draw Conclusions**

3. As you read, what questions did you ask, and how did they help you better understand the selection? **Ask Questions**

4. William used a *clearing, pegs,* a *cellar,* and *barrels* to solve problems in his new home. Make a list. Write each word and tell how William used the item. **Vocabulary**

**Look Back and Write** Look back at page 262. What did William do to keep the roof from caving in? Use details from the selection to write your answer. Draw a diagram if it will help your explanation.

**Meet author Ginger Howard on page 412.**

266

# Write Now

## Explanatory Paragraph

**Prompt**

In *William's House*, special features make a house suitable for its environment. Think about the features that help your home fit into its environment. Now write an explanatory paragraph about those features.

**Student Model**

Main idea is stated in first sentence. ———•

We live in a house built for the Arizona desert. Summer days are hot, but air conditioning keeps our house cool. We have thick walls made of stucco. This keeps warm air inside in winter and cool air inside in summer. Our floors are made of tiles. They feel cool on bare feet, even on hot summer days. We have a big patio. Fresh breezes blow across it on summer evenings, so we sit there to keep cool. Winter nights get chilly, so we have a cozy fireplace in our living room. Our house fits perfectly in the Arizona desert.

Writer stays <u>focused</u> on main **idea** and uses facts to support that idea.

Last sentence sums up main idea. ———•

**Use the model to help you write your own explanatory paragraph.**

267

### Expository Nonfiction

#### Genre

- Expository nonfiction explains facts about objects or ideas.

- It often requires careful reading.

#### Text Features

- Photographs with captions are often included to help the reader understand.

- Graphics, such as a time line, sometimes provide additional information.

#### Link to Social Studies

Use the library or the Internet to research log cabins. Find out about the inside of log cabins.

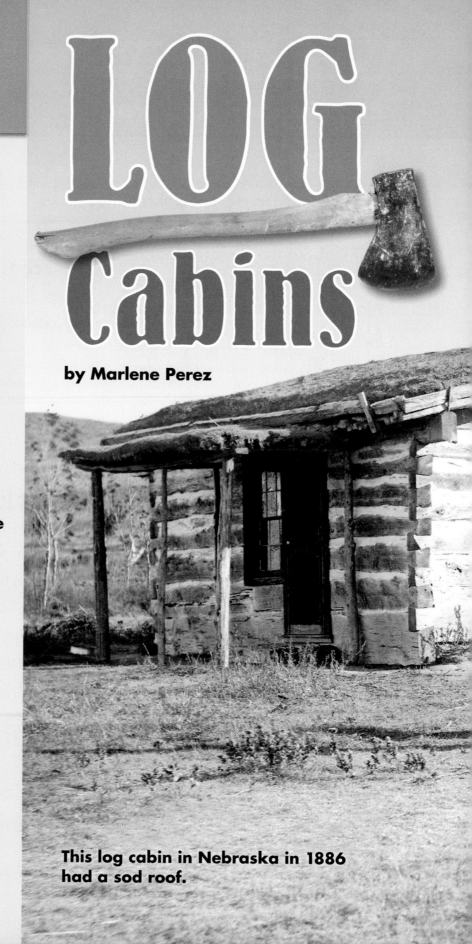

# LOG Cabins

by Marlene Perez

This log cabin in Nebraska in 1886 had a sod roof.

When people moved west in the 1800s, there were no houses or towns or shops. They couldn't bring many supplies along when they journeyed into the wild. They had to think of ways to build houses using what was around them.

Settlers from Europe built the first log cabins in the United States. These were square, one-room cabins. To add more room, a loft with a ladder might be added. Some cabins were made of round logs. Settlers closed the space between the logs with mud, shells from the river, or even cow manure.

**Ask Questions** What questions did you have as you read this page?

Later, cabins were made with logs cut to fit together better. The logs were cut flat and the ends were notched. The logs were stacked in an interlocking pattern. This made the houses sturdier and easier to build.

Flat logs were notched at the ends. They fit together tightly.

Settlers made do with what they had available. Some log cabins had roofs made of grass sod or cedar planks. Log cabin floors and chimneys were made of stone or rock, which settlers found in the wilderness. Some cabins had floors of dirt, which had been pounded flat. Other floors were made of logs that were laid flat. These log floors were called *puncheons*.

In 1862, a law was passed that gave settlers a piece of land for free if they would build a house, live there, and farm the land for five years. The log cabin was a good choice for a home. It could be built quickly. Trees from the forests could be used for logs. A log cabin didn't need nails, which were expensive and hard to find. Settlers could build a log cabin using a few simple tools, such as an ax and an auger.

When the railroad grew and pushed its way west, people could then buy lumber from mills. Wood-framed houses

**1804**
Lewis and
Clark begin
exploration.

**1842**
Pioneers travel
Oregon Trail
westward.

**1869**
Transcontinental
railroad
is finished.

**1830**
Work begins
on railroads.

**1862**
Law passed to give
settlers free land.

replaced log cabins. Often, homeowners tore down the cabins and reused the lumber to build bigger houses.

Over the years, American homes changed from one-room cabins to larger, sturdier buildings. But because of the clever way it was first made, the log cabin will always be a symbol of American creativity.

## Reading Across Texts

When it was finished, how was William's house different from the early log cabins you read about in this article?

## Writing Across Texts

Write a short paragraph telling which house you would rather live in and why.

**Draw Conclusions**  What happened to log cabins after the railroad came?

# Ants

**by Marilyn Singer**

One and one and one and one
  Dead leaves
  Dead crickets
One ant alone can't pick it
  up
  can't drag this meal to our busy nest
But one and one and one and one
  Together we tow
  Together we know
any time of day this is so:
One and one and one and one
  is the best way
  to get things done

# The Sure-Footed Shoe Finder

**by Andrea Perry**

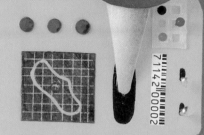

How many times has this happened to you?
You're late for the school bus and can't find a shoe.
It might take you hours unless you have got
The Sure-Footed Shoe Finder there on the spot!

Just lift up the lever and open the gate,
then toss in the shoe that is missing its mate.
With a beep and a clang and a stagger and lurch,
the Shoe Finder's off on its shoe-finding search.

The powerful Foot-Odor-Sensitive Vent
tracks down your sneaker by matching its scent,
and mere seconds later the shoe is retrieved.
You won't miss the school bus! Now aren't
you relieved?

Most of our customers happen to choose
our standard shoe model for footwear they lose,
although the new jumbo Shoe Finder can trace
even those snow boots you children misplace!

# Third-Grade GENIUS

by Gary Soto

Me, I took two wires, a battery, and a bulb
And fit them nicely together in my hand.

Show and tell.

I said, "I know about electricity."
Then I walked up and down the aisles,
     showing my invention,
A flashlight of sorts. This on a rainy day,
With the battery of the sun gone dead.
This on a day when the headlights of cars
     came on at noon.

Me, I showed my friends about electricity,
The beam of my invention glinting off the
     teacher's glasses.
I beamed it at the hamster, whose eyes glowed
     red as berries.

I sat down, a magician who brought light
    to the classroom.
I kicked my legs, ropes hanging from
    the chair.
I was happy.

School ended.
The rain started to throw darts on our
    shoulders.
But I didn't worry. I had a baseball cap
And my invention in my hand,
The one-eyed headlight that brightened
    the sidewalk
On the way back home.

275

# Wrap-Up

## Tale of a Problem Solver

In *Prudy's Problem* and *Tops & Bottoms,* you read about some characters and their clever solutions to problems. Write a folk tale or an animal story about a clever solution to a different problem. You can begin by completing a story map.

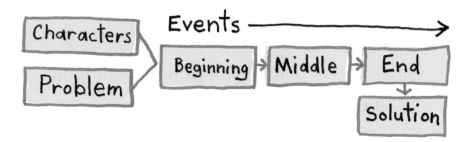

# What are smart ways that problems are solved?

connect to
**SCIENCE**

## Real-World Comics

Just like the penguins in *Penguin Chick*, people, plants, and other animals must find ways to adapt to problems in their environments. Make a comic strip about a real event in nature. Show how a person, plant, or animal adapts to find a solution.

connect to
**SOCIAL STUDIES**

## Better Homes and Other Buildings

In *William's House*, William made many changes to his home so that it would better protect his family. How could you change the design of a building in your community so that people in it would be better protected and more comfortable? Draw a plan for the building or construct a model.

UNIT 3

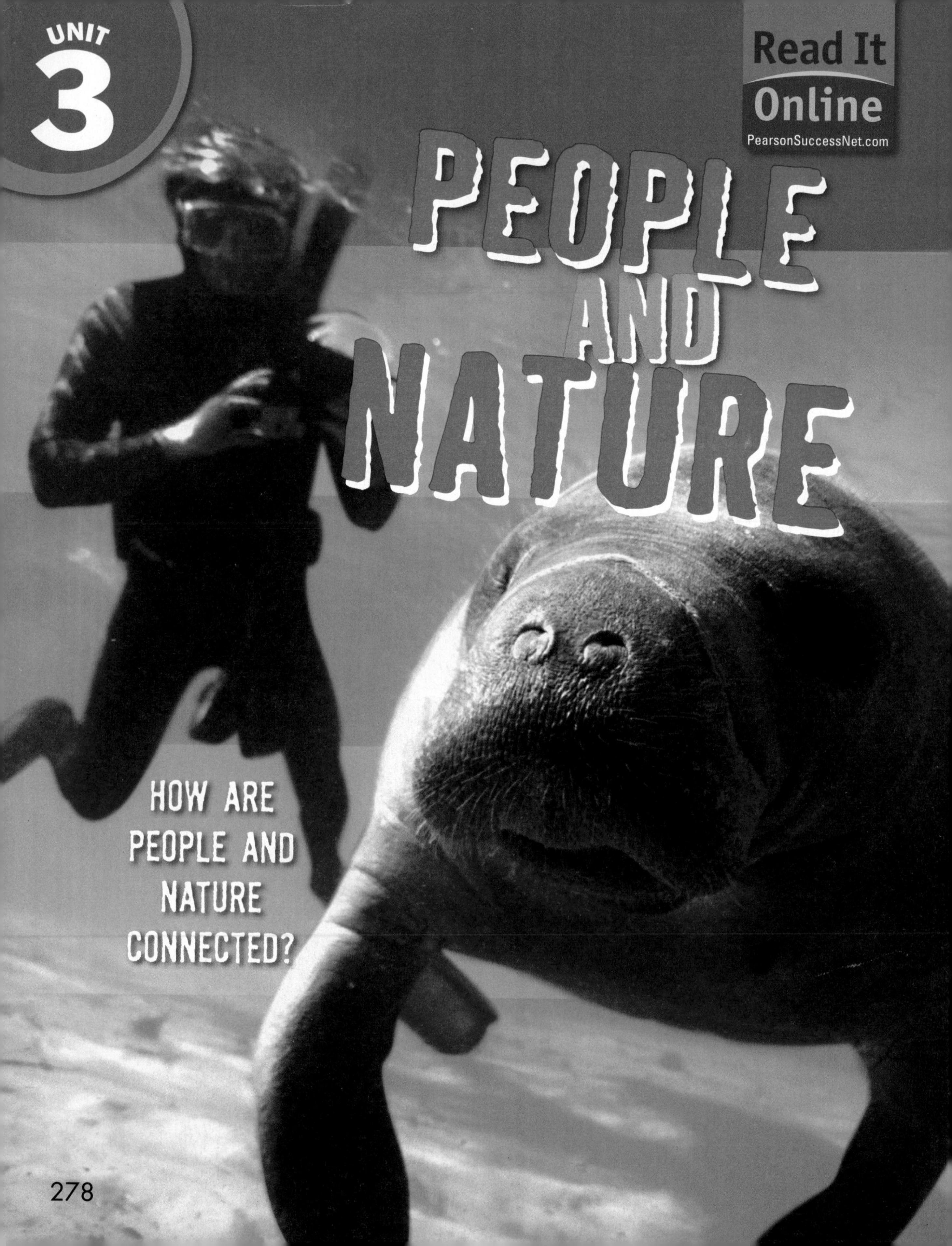


# PEOPLE AND NATURE

HOW ARE PEOPLE AND NATURE CONNECTED?

**Skill**
Cause and Effect

**Strategy**
Story Structure

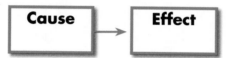

# Cause and Effect

- A cause tells *why* something happened.

- An effect is *what* happened.

- Words such as *because* and *so* are clues that can help you figure out a cause and its effect.

| Cause | → | Effect |
|-------|---|--------|

- Sometimes a cause has more than one effect.

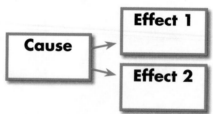

 **Strategy: Story Structure**

A story has a beginning, a middle, and an end. This means that events happen all along the way. One event leads to the next. Good readers use this structure to find causes and their effects.

## Write to Read

1. Read "Winter Blooms." Make graphic organizers like those above. Note at least three causes and their effects.

2. Use your graphic organizer to write a paragraph that explains three effects of Margo reading the book. Use clue words.

# Winter Blooms

Margo loved flowers. They made her think of spring. There were no flowers growing in the yard now because it was January and the ground was frozen. Margo wondered how to grow flowers in her house, so she went to the library for a book.

She read the book carefully so she would know how to make flowers grow in her house. The book had a list of what she needed for an indoor garden, so she went to the garden shop to buy some supplies. The book said flowers grow best near a window because they need plenty of sun. So, she set her new green plants on her kitchen windowsill. The book also said that flowers need water. Margo put the watering can near the sink to remind her to water the plants often. She looked at her dreary yard and then at her cheerful pots of plants. She hoped they would bloom soon!

**Skill** There are some clue words in this paragraph —*because* and *so*. What causes and effects can you find in this paragraph?

**Strategy** Here's another clue word. This sentence is like the one in the first paragraph. This pattern should help you recognize that events are happening in order and that they affect one another.

## Words to Know

- bulbs
- sprouting
- blooming
- recognizing
- beauty
- humor
- showers
- doze

**Remember**

Try the strategy. Then, if you need more help, use your glossary or a dictionary.

# Vocabulary Strategy
## for Endings

**Word Structure** Sometimes when you are reading, you may come across a word you don't know. Look closely at the word. Does it have -s at the end? The ending -s is often added to a noun to make the word plural, or mean more than one. Try to use the ending to help you figure out the meaning of the word.

**1.** Put your finger over the -s ending.

**2.** Look at the base word. (That's the word without the ending.) Do you know what the base word means?

**3.** Try your meaning in the sentence. Does it make sense?

Read "Bulbs to Blooms." Look for words that have the -s ending. Use the ending to help you figure out the meanings of the words.

# Bulbs to Blooms

Every fall Mr. Connor plants bulbs in his yard. The bulbs look like big, ugly brown lumps. It's hard to imagine them sprouting roots and stems and becoming plants. Yet, in early spring dozens of tulips and daffodils will be blooming in Mr. Connor's yard. It is a wonderful sight. Mr. Connor has won awards recognizing his yard for its beauty. He is very proud of his bulbs. Fortunately, he also has a sense of humor.

One day last fall, I was sitting on the porch with my dog Max. Rain showers had made the ground wet and soft. Mr. Connor had just finished planting his bulbs. I told Max to stay on the porch with me. He was playing with his toys. I was reading a book. Then I started to doze. When I woke up, Max was in Mr. Connor's yard, digging up the bulbs! I was horrified, but Mr. Connor just laughed. He said he could have used a good hole digger. Then I helped him replant the bulbs.

## Words to Write

Imagine what Mr. Connor's yard looks like in the spring. Write a description of it. Use words from the Words to Know list.

# The Gardener

by Sarah Stewart

illustrated by David Small

 **Genre** **Realistic fiction** is a made-up story that could happen in real life. What parts of this selection could really happen?

Who is this gardener, and what
does she do that is special?

August 27, 1935

Dear Uncle Jim,

   Grandma told us after supper that you want me to come to the city and live with you until things get better. Did she tell you that Papa has been out of work for a long time, and no one asks Mama to make dresses anymore?

   We all cried, even Papa. But then Mama made us laugh with her stories about your chasing her up trees when you were both little. Did you really do that?

   I'm small, but strong, and I'll help you all I can. However, Grandma said to finish my schoolwork before doing anything else.

                    Your niece,
                    Lydia Grace Finch

September 3, 1935

Dear Uncle Jim,

    I'm mailing this from the train station. I forgot to tell you in the last letter *three important things* that I'm too shy to say to your face:

    1. I know a lot about gardening, but nothing about baking.

    2. I'm anxious to learn to bake, but is there any place to plant seeds?

    3. I like to be called "Lydia Grace"—just like Grandma.

       Your niece,
       Lydia Grace Finch

On the train
September 4, 1935
Dear Mama,
   I feel so pretty in your dress that you made over for me. I hope you don't miss it too much.

Dear Papa,
   I haven't forgotten what you said about recognizing Uncle Jim: "Just look for Mama's face with a big nose and a mustache!" I promise not to tell him. (Does he have a sense of humor?)

And, dearest Grandma,
   Thank you for the seeds. The train is rocking me to sleep, and every time I doze off, I dream of gardens.
        Love to all,
        Lydia Grace

September 5, 1935

Dear Mama, Papa, and Grandma,

    I'm so excited!!!

    There are window boxes here! They look as if they've been waiting for me, so now we'll both wait for spring.

    And, Grandma, the sun shines down on the corner where I'll live and work.

        Love to all,

        Lydia Grace

P.S. Uncle Jim doesn't smile.

December 25, 1935

Dear Mama, Papa, and Grandma,

I adore the seed catalogues you sent for Christmas. And, Grandma, thank you for all the bulbs. I hope you received my drawings.

I wrote a long poem for Uncle Jim. He didn't smile, but I think he liked it. He read it aloud, then put it in his shirt pocket and patted it.

Love to all,
Lydia Grace

February 12, 1936

Dearest Grandma,

Thank you again for those bulbs you sent at Christmas. You should see them now!

I really like Ed and Emma Beech, Uncle Jim's friends who work here. When I first arrived, Emma told me she'd show me how to knead bread if I would teach her the Latin names of all the flowers I know. Now, just half a year later, I'm kneading bread and she's speaking Latin!

More good news: We have a store cat named Otis who at this very moment is sleeping at the foot of *my* bed.

Love to all,
Lydia Grace

P.S. Uncle Jim isn't smiling yet, but I'm hoping for a smile soon.

March 5, 1936

Dear Mama, Papa, and Grandma,

   I've discovered a secret place. You can't imagine how wonderful it is. No one else knows about it but Otis.

   I have great plans.

   Thank you for all the letters. I'll try to write more, but I'm really busy planting all your seeds in cracked teacups and bent cake pans! And, Grandma, you should smell the good dirt I'm bringing home from the vacant lot down the street.

           Love to all,
           Lydia Grace

April 27, 1936

Dearest Grandma,

All the seeds and roots are sprouting. I can hear you saying, "April showers bring May flowers."

Emma and I are sprucing up the bakery and I'm playing a great trick on Uncle Jim. He sees me reading my mail, planting seeds in the window boxes, going to school, doing my homework, sweeping the floor. But he never sees me working in my secret place.

Love to all,
Lydia Grace

P.S. I'm planning on a big smile from Uncle Jim in the near future.

May 27, 1936

Dear Mama, Papa, and Grandma,

You should have heard Emma laugh today when I opened your letter and dirt fell out onto the sidewalk! Thank you for all the baby plants. They survived the trip in the big envelope.

More about Emma: She's helping me with the secret place. Hurrah!

Love to all,
Lydia Grace

P.S. I saw Uncle Jim almost smile today. The store was full (well, *almost* full) of customers.

June 27, 1936

Dear Grandma,

    Flowers are blooming all over the place. I'm also growing radishes, onions, and three kinds of lettuce in the window boxes.

    Some neighbors have brought containers for me to fill with flowers, and a few customers even gave me plants from their gardens this spring! They don't call me "Lydia Grace" anymore. They call me "the gardener."

           Love to all,

           Lydia Grace

    P.S. I'm sure Uncle Jim will smile soon. I'm almost ready to show him the secret place.

July 4, 1936

Dearest Mama, Papa, and Grandma,

I am bursting with happiness! The entire city seems so beautiful, especially this morning.

The secret place is ready for Uncle Jim. At noon, the store will close for the holiday, and then we'll bring him up to the roof.

I've tried to remember everything you ever taught me about beauty.

Love to all,

Lydia Grace

P.S. I can already imagine Uncle Jim's smile.

July 11, 1936

Dear Mama, Papa, and Grandma,

My heart is pounding so hard I'm sure the customers can hear it downstairs!

At lunch today, Uncle Jim put the "Closed" sign on the door and told Ed and Emma and me to go upstairs and wait. He appeared with the most amazing cake I've ever seen—covered in flowers!

I truly believe that cake equals one thousand smiles.

And then he took your letter out of his pocket with the news of Papa's job!

I'M COMING HOME!

Love to all, and see you soon,
Lydia Grace

P.S. Grandma, I've given all of my plants to Emma. I can't wait to help you in your garden again. We gardeners never retire.

# Reader Response

**Open for Discussion** Lydia Grace certainly makes the best of things. Some people would say that when life handed her a lemon, she made lemonade. Tell some ways in which Lydia Grace shows she is that kind of person.

**1.** The author writes this story in the form of letters. What did you think of this way of writing? What kind of information can you get from a letter? **Think Like an Author**

**2.** What effect did Lydia Grace's visit have on Uncle Jim? Why do you think so? **Cause and Effect**

**3.** What was Lydia Grace trying to achieve when she first arrived at Uncle Jim's? By the end of the story, did she succeed? **Story Structure**

**4.** Uncle Jim's customers began calling Lydia Grace "the gardener." Explain this new name. Use words from the Words to Know list. **Vocabulary**

**Look Back and Write** Lydia Grace writes a poem for Uncle Jim. How did he feel about the poem? How do you know? Look back at page 290. Use details from the story in your answer.

**Meet author Sarah Stewart on page 410 and illustrator David Small on page 421.**

# Write Now

## Journal Entry

**Prompt**

*The Gardener* describes a special garden. Think about a special place in nature. Now write a journal entry about that place, using vivid words.

**Writing Trait**

Vivid **word choice** helps readers picture a setting. Use words that appeal to the senses.

**Student Model**

Writer expresses feelings in the first sentence.

Vivid <u>word choice</u> appeals to readers' senses.

Writer engages readers in the final sentence.

I love the beach on a summer day. All I see is white sand, dark blue water, and light blue sky. The sea gulls screech above, and the ocean roars in the background. I smell the salty air and suntan lotion. The sand feels warm and scratchy under my bare feet, and the ocean breeze feels fresh on my face. When I finally get the nerve to go in the water, it feels like ice. Cold waves startle me, but soon I can feel the hot sun on my skin. The water feels refreshing, and the waves have a gentle rhythm. Come join me at my special place.

**Use the model to help you write your own journal entry.**

# Worms at Work

## How-to Article

### Genre

- A how-to article explains how to do or make something.

- A good how-to article lists the materials you will need and explains the steps you will take.

### Text Features

- This article has three sections, each containing different information. As you read, think about the purpose of each section.

- Watch for numbered lists. How do they help?

### Link to Science

Use reference materials to find out more about an earthworm's body. Draw and label a picture of one.

by Ann Weil

Did you know that people all over the world keep worms to change their garbage into rich soil called *compost?* Worms eat food scraps. Two pounds of worms can eat a pound of garbage every day. That's a lot of trash.

Keeping worms is easy. It can also be a lot of fun. And while you're having fun taking care of the worms, you're also helping our environment by recycling trash into compost for houseplants and gardens.

Here's what you need to do.

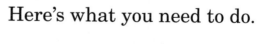

# You will need:

- Red worms ·················O
  (also called red wigglers)

You can start with as few as **50–100** worms, but more worms will eat more garbage. Some garden stores sell worms by the pound. One pound of worms contains **1,000–1,500** worms.

- A large plastic container, about 12 inches deep

**12"**

- Plastic bag or loose cover for the container

- Newspaper, leaves, and soil to make the bedding

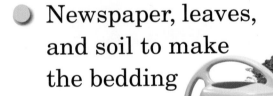

## Feeding Dos

**YES:** Eggshells; coffee grounds and used tea bags; cooked rice, pasta, or potatoes; cereals; fruit and vegetable peelings; bread

- Water

## Feeding Don'ts

**NO:** Meat and fish, dairy products. Worms would eat these, but they may make the worm bin smell bad and attract rats and flies.

- Food scraps ···············O

**Cause and Effect**    What happens when you put worms in with food scraps?

# Making Your Worm Bin

**1** **Prepare the container.**
Poke small holes through the bottom of the container.

**2** **Prepare the bedding.** ·········O

Fill the container about three-quarters full with small pieces of torn newspaper. (Do not use any colored or shiny newspaper.)

Add about a handful of soil. You can put in some dead leaves, too, if you like.

**3** **Pour water on the bedding.** ·····················O
Make sure all the bedding is damp, but not soaking wet.

**4** **Add the worms.**
Gently move the worms into their new home.

**5** **Feed the worms.** ············O

Bury the food scraps in the bedding.

**6** **Cover the bin.**
Make sure air can still move in and around the bin.

---

**Text Structure**    Are these steps easy to follow? Why?

# Maintaining Your Worm Bin

**1 Keep the bedding moist.**
Make sure the bedding does not dry out.

**2 Feed the worms.** ⋯⋯⋯○
Pay attention to how much the worms are eating. If they are not eating all the scraps, feed them less.

**3 Harvest the compost.** ⋯⋯⋯○
Worms eat their bedding as well as their food. When the bedding is mostly gone, push what's left to one side and add fresh, damp bedding to the other side. Bury the food scraps in the new bedding. The worms will move to the food so you can harvest the compost without taking all the worms with it.

**4 Use the compost!**
Compost helps plants grow better. Add it to potted houseplants or to your outdoor flower or vegetable garden.

### Reading Across Texts
You have read *The Gardener* and "Worms at Work." What do both selections tell about taking care of a garden?

**Writing Across Texts** Make a list of helpful things that worms do for us.

Pushing Up the Sky

**Comprehension**

**Skill**
Author's Purpose

**Strategy**
Summarize

 **Skill**

# Author's Purpose

- The author's purpose is the reason an author writes something.

- An author may be trying to persuade, to inform, to entertain, or to express ideas and feelings.

- Different parts of a piece of writing may have different purposes.

|  | Purpose | Why do you think so? |
|---|---|---|
| Beginning |  |  |
| Middle |  |  |
| End |  |  |

 **Strategy**

## Strategy: Summarize

Summing up the main ideas and details as you read can help you figure out the author's purpose. For example, are you reading facts that explain something? Then the purpose is probably to inform.

# Write to Read

**1.** Read "An Up-and-Down Story." Make a graphic organizer like the one above. Choose the main purpose for each part of the article. Explain your choice.

**2.** Write a short summary of "An Up-and-Down Story." Then explain what the author's main purpose was and why you think that.

# An UP-and-DOWN Story

In Olympia, Washington, you will find a tall pole. However, this pole is not just any pole. It is a story pole.

A story pole is different from a totem pole. A totem pole tells about a family. A story pole uses animal stories to teach children about their culture and responsibility. The story pole in Olympia has 21 carved figures on it. Each teaches a lesson about life.

The story pole was made by Snohomish Chief William Shelton. It was carved from a great cedar tree. Chief Shelton worked on the pole for five years. When he died in 1938, other people in his tribe finished the carving.

In 1940 the pole was done, but there was no money to put it up. Children from around the state each gave one cent. Together, they raised enough money.

If you are ever in Olympia, be sure to visit the story pole. You will learn about the Snohomish culture. And you will see a beautiful work of art.

**Strategy** Here is a good place to stop and sum up what you have read so far. This paragraph explains what a story pole is.

**Skill** This paragraph is about how Chief Shelton made the story pole. The author's purpose is probably to inform us about story poles. Read on. Does the purpose change?

## Words to Know

overhead

poked

imagined

narrator

antlers

languages

# Vocabulary Strategy
## for Unfamiliar Words

**Glossary** Sometimes you can use a glossary to find out the meaning of a word. The important words in a book are often listed in a glossary. A glossary is a list of words and their meanings. The words are listed in alphabetical order. A glossary is usually at the back of the book.

**1.** Turn to the glossary in the book.

**2.** Use the first letters in the word to help you find the word in the glossary.

**3.** Read the meaning of the word. Then try the meaning in the sentence. Does it make sense?

As you read "The Class Play," use the glossary to find the meanings of the vocabulary words.

# The Class Play

"I have counted the votes," declared Ms. Chavez, waving a sheet of paper overhead. "Our play for Parents Night will be *Pushing Up the Sky.* Tryouts are tomorrow."

Jenna grinned and poked Kate in the shoulder. They both wanted to be Chiefs together. They had already learned the lines and planned their costumes.

The next day Jenna tried out for the First Chief. That was scarier than she had imagined. She forgot several words.

When Kate tried out for the Seventh Chief's part, she didn't make a single mistake.

Later, Ms. Chavez announced the parts. Kate was the Narrator. She had a lot of lines, but she didn't get to wear a costume. "But I made such a beautiful cape," she wailed.

Jenna was the Elk. She didn't have any lines at all, and she had to wear brown paper antlers on her head. "Don't elks know *any* languages?"

Both girls were disappointed but glad to be in the play. Maybe next time they would get the parts they wanted.

## Words to Write

Imagine that you are Ms. Chavez. What would you say to Jenna and Kate? Write your response. Use as many words from the Words to Know list as you can.

# Pushing Up

by Joseph Bruchac

illustrated by Teresa Flavin

Genre

A **play** uses a cast of characters. Look at the characters in *Pushing Up the Sky* and think about which role you would like to play.

# the Sky

*What would happen if you could touch the sky?*

# Snohomish

The Snohomish people live in the area of the Northwest that is now known as the state of Washington, not far from Puget Sound. They fished in the ocean and gathered food from the shore. Their homes and many of the things they used every day, such as bowls and canoe paddles, were carved from the trees. Like many of the other peoples of the area, they also carved totem poles, which recorded the history and stories of their nation. This story is one that was carved into a totem pole made for the city of Everett, Washington, by Chief William Shelton.

## Characters

### Speaking Roles

NARRATOR

TALL MAN

GIRL

MOTHER

BOY

FIRST CHIEF

SECOND CHIEF

THIRD CHIEF

FOURTH CHIEF

FIFTH CHIEF

SIXTH CHIEF

SEVENTH CHIEF

## Non-speaking Roles

Animals and Birds—as many as group size will accommodate. Animals familiar to the Snohomish would include Dog, Deer, Elk, Mountain Goat, Bear, Mountain Lion, Rabbit, Weasel, Wolf, and Fox. Birds would include Hawk, Bald Eagle, Golden Eagle, Jay, Seagull, Raven, Heron, and Kingfisher.

## Props/Scenery

**The village** can be suggested with a painted backdrop showing houses made of cedar planks among tall fir trees and redwoods, with the ocean visible in the background. Potted plants can be added around the stage to suggest trees if desired.

**Bows and arrows** held by Boy in Scene I can be from a toy set or made from cardboard.

**The poles** held by people and animals in Scene III can be rulers or long tubes of cardboard.

## Costumes

**People,** including the **Narrator,** can wear blankets or towels. **Chiefs** wear them around their shoulders, and other humans wear them wrapped around their waists to suggest the robes often worn by people of the Northwest. Cone-shaped hats (worn by Snohomish women) may be worn by girls playing human characters.

Depending on their number and type, the **Animals** can be suggested by face paint or with decorated masks made from paper plates.

# Scene I: A Village Among Many Tall Trees

*(Tall Man, Girl, Mother, and Boy stand onstage.)*

**NARRATOR:** Long ago the sky was very close to the earth. The sky was so close that some people could jump right into it. Those people who were not good jumpers could climb up the tall fir trees and step into the sky. But people were not happy that the sky was so close to the earth. Tall people kept bumping their heads on the sky. And there were other problems.

**TALL MAN:** Oh, that hurt! I just hit my head on the sky again.

**GIRL:** I just threw my ball, and it landed in the sky, and I can't get it back.

**MOTHER:** Where is my son? Has he climbed a tree and gone up into the sky again?

**BOY:** Every time I shoot my bow, my arrows get stuck in the sky!

**ALL:** THE SKY IS TOO CLOSE!

313

# Scene II: The Same Village

*(The seven chiefs stand together onstage.)*

**NARRATOR:** So people decided something had to be done. A great meeting was held for all the different tribes. The seven wisest chiefs got together to talk about the problem.

**FIRST CHIEF:** My people all think the sky is too close.

**SECOND CHIEF:** The Creator did a very good job of making the world.

**THIRD CHIEF:** That is true, but the Creator should have put the sky up higher. My tall son keeps hitting his head on the sky.

**FOURTH CHIEF:** My daughter keeps losing her ball in the sky.

**FIFTH CHIEF:** People keep going up into the sky when they should be staying on the earth to help each other.

**SIXTH CHIEF:** When mothers look for their children, they cannot find them because they are up playing in the sky.

**SEVENTH CHIEF:** We are agreed, then. The sky is too close.

**ALL:** WE ARE AGREED.

**SECOND CHIEF:** What can we do?

**SEVENTH CHIEF:** I have an idea. Let's push up the sky.

**THIRD CHIEF:** The sky is heavy.

**SEVENTH CHIEF:** If we all push together, we can do it.

**SIXTH CHIEF:** We will ask the birds and animals to help. They also do not like it that the sky is so close.

**SECOND CHIEF:** The elk are always getting their antlers caught in the sky.

**FOURTH CHIEF:** The birds are always hitting their wings on it.

**FIRST CHIEF:** We will cut tall trees to make poles. We can use those poles to push up the sky.

**FIFTH CHIEF:** That is a good idea. Are we all agreed?

**ALL:** WE ARE ALL AGREED.

# Scene III: The Same Village

*(All the People, except Seventh Chief, are gathered together. They hold long poles. The Birds and Animals are with them. They all begin pushing randomly, jabbing their poles into the air. The sky can be imagined as just above them.)*

**GIRL:** It isn't working.

**BOY:** The sky is still too close.

**FIFTH CHIEF:** Where is Seventh Chief? This was his idea!

**SEVENTH CHIEF** *(entering)*: Here I am. I had to find this long pole.

**FIRST CHIEF:** Your plan is not good! See, we are pushing and the sky is not moving.

**SEVENTH CHIEF:** Ah, but I said we must push together.

**FIFTH CHIEF:** We need a signal so that all can push together. Our people speak different languages.

**SEVENTH CHIEF:** Let us use YAH-HOO as the signal. Ready?

**ALL:** YES!

**SEVENTH CHIEF:** YAH-HOO.

*(At the signal, everyone pushes together.)*

**ALL:** YAH-HOO!

**SEVENTH CHIEF:** YAH-HOO.

*(Again everyone pushes together.)*

**ALL:** YAH-HOO!

**TALL MAN:** We are doing it!

**MOTHER:** Now my son won't be able to hide in the sky!

**SEVENTH CHIEF:** YAH-HOO.

*(Again everyone pushes together.)*

**ALL:** YAH-HOO!

**BOY:** It will be too high for my arrows to stick into it.

**SEVENTH CHIEF:** YAH-HOO.

*(Again everyone pushes together.)*

**ALL:** YAH-HOOOO!

**FIRST CHIEF:** We have done it!

**NARRATOR:** So the sky was pushed up. It was done by everyone working together. That night, though, when everyone looked overhead, they saw many stars in the sky. The stars were shining through the holes poked into the sky by the poles of everyone who pushed it up higher.

No one ever bumped his head on the sky again. And those stars are there to this day.

# Reader Response

**Open for Discussion** Stage directors use sound effects and movements to help a play seem real for the audience. What sound effects and movements would you put into this play to help it seem real?

1. When does the narrator talk in this play? Why do you think the author includes a narrator? **Think Like an Author**

2. The author's purpose is the writer's reason for writing. Give one important purpose the author might have for writing *Pushing Up the Sky*. **Author's Purpose**

3. If someone asked you what *Pushing Up the Sky* is about, how would you summarize it for them? Think about the problem the tribes have and how they solve it to help with your summary. **Summarize**

4. *Narrator* is a word that often appears in plays. What other words in the story are "play words"? **Vocabulary**

**Look Back and Write** How does this play explain something in nature? Write what it is and how the people explained it. Use details from the play to support your answer.

Meet author **Joseph Bruchac on page 413.**

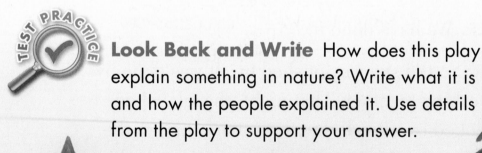

# Write Now

## Skit

**Prompt**

*Pushing Up the Sky* tells about people working together to do something important. Think about a real or imaginary time when a group worked together.
Now write a skit about that time.

> **Writing Trait**
>
> Correct use of **conventions** (spelling, capitalization, punctuation, grammar) makes a skit easy to read.

**Student Model**

**Narrator sets the scene.** →

NARRATOR: The people who live on Oakwood loved their city street. But in the summer they wished they had a vegetable garden.

MR. RUIZ: I will use my mower to cut the grass on this vacant lot. (He makes mowing motions.)

MS. LEE: I will plant vegetable seeds in neat rows. (She pokes holes and puts in seeds.)

THREE KIDS: We will pull up the weeds around the vegetable plants. (They pull weeds.)

MR. THOMAS: I will gather the vegetables. (He picks vegetables.)

MRS. JAY AND MRS. FONG: We will cook a vegetable feast.

EVERYBODY: We will all eat a delicious meal!

> Writer uses <u>conventions</u> for skits: characters' names are capitalized and followed by colons. Stage directions are underlined and in parentheses.

**Use this model to help you write your own skit.**

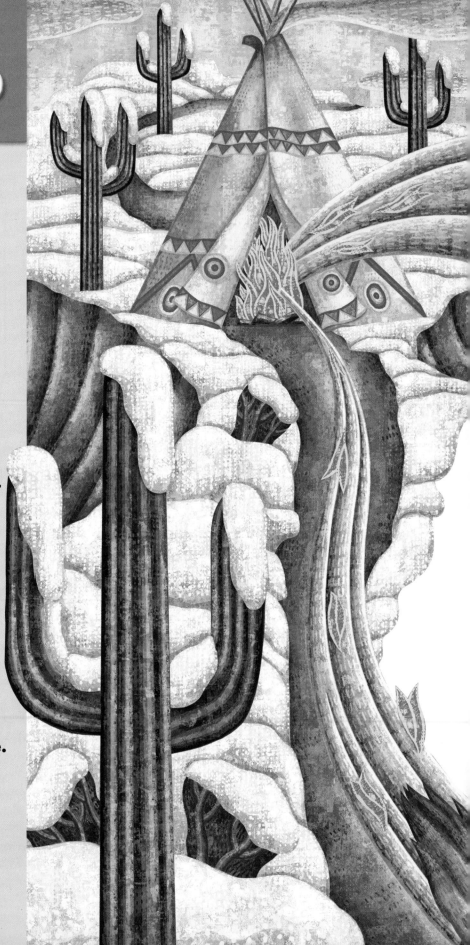

## Myth

### Genre

- Myths are old stories that have been told orally for generations.

- Myths often explore events in nature.

- The animal characters act like people. They can talk and think.

- The author capitalizes each animal's name. This way, one character represents all the animals of that kind. As you read, look for how the author uses that one character to show why all the animals of its kind look a certain way.

### Link to Reading

Look in the library for other myths about nature. Share these stories with your class.

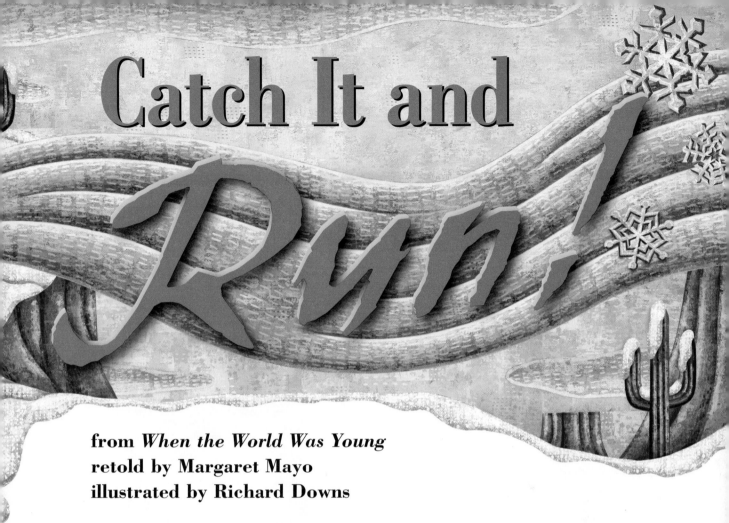

# Catch It and Run!

**from *When the World Was Young***
**retold by Margaret Mayo**
**illustrated by Richard Downs**

A long, long time ago, all fire belonged to three
Fire Beings who kept it hidden in their tepee, high on a
mountaintop. They would not share the fire with anyone
and guarded it carefully, night and day. So, when winter
came and the fierce winds howled and snow covered the
earth, men, women, and children had no way of warming
themselves. No fire. No hot food. Nothing at all.

Now Coyote, who is wise, knew about fire, and
one year, at winter's end, when he saw how cold and
miserable the people were, he decided to steal some
fire and give it to them. But how would he do it?

**C Summarize** Explain the problem that has been introduced.

Coyote thought hard.

He called a meeting of the animals, and he said, "Who will help me steal some fire and give it to the people?" And Bear, Deer, Squirrel, Chipmunk, and Frog offered to help.

Coyote thought again.

"Bear," he said, "you are big and strong, so you must come with me to the Fire Beings' tepee. Deer, Squirrel, and Chipmunk, you are fast runners, so you must wait beside the trail, ready to run."

"What about me?" asked Frog. "I'd like to help!"

"Fro-og," sighed Coyote, shaking his head, "you're such a squatty little thing. You can jump and swim. But you can't run. There's nothing you can do."

"I could wait by the pond and be ready," said Frog. "Just in case. . . ."

"You do that," said Coyote. "Wait and be ready. Just in case. . . ."

That made Frog happy. He squatted down by the pond, and he waited while the others set off along the trail through the forest that led to the Fire Beings' mountaintop.

On the way Coyote stopped from time to time and told one of the animals to wait beside the trail. First Squirrel, next Chipmunk, and then Deer were left behind, and at last Bear and Coyote walked on alone.

**Summarize** What is Coyote's plan so far?

When they reached the tepee on top of the
mountain, Coyote told Bear to wait in the shadows until
he heard Coyote call *"Aooo!"* Then Bear must make
a big, loud rumpus.

Coyote crept up to the tepee. He gave a soft bark, and
one of the Fire Beings opened the flap and looked out.

Coyote sort of trembled and said in his quietest,
most polite voice, "My legs are freezing cold. May I
please put them inside your warm tepee?"

He was so exceedingly polite that the Fire Being
said, "Ye-es, all right. . . ."

Coyote stepped in his front legs, then he stepped
in his back legs, and then he whisked in his tail. He
looked longingly at the great blazing fire in the center
of the tepee, but he said nothing. He just lay down and
closed his eyes as if he were going to sleep. But the
next moment he gave a long Coyote call, *"Aooo-ooo!"*

From outside the tepee came the sound of a big,
loud rumpus as Bear growled and stamped about.

The Fire Beings all rushed out shouting, "Who's
that?" And when they saw Bear, they chased him.

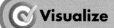 **Visualize**   Create a picture in your mind of the loud rumpus Bear makes.

Coyote was ready. He grabbed a piece of burning wood between his teeth and away he ran, out of the tepee and down the mountain.

As soon as the Fire Beings saw Coyote with the firebrand, they abandoned Bear and chased Coyote.

Coyote ran and ran. He was fast, but the Fire Beings were faster, and they came closer.

Then Coyote saw Deer. "Catch it and *run!*" he called and threw the firebrand.

Deer caught it and ran. But he ran so fast that the wind fanned the fire out behind him, and a flame jumped onto his long tail and burned most of it. So that's why Deer has a shortish tail, even today.

Deer was fast, but the Fire Beings were faster, and they came closer.

Then Deer saw Chipmunk. "Catch it and *run!*" he called and threw the firebrand.

Chipmunk caught it and ran. But the Fire Beings came closer and closer, until one of them reached out an arm and clawed his back and left three long black stripes. And that's why Chipmunk has stripes on his back, even today.

Then Chipmunk saw Squirrel. "Catch it and *run!*" he called and threw the firebrand.

Squirrel caught it and ran. But the firebrand had been burning fast, and it was now so short that its great heat made Squirrel's bushy tail curl up over his back. And that's why Squirrel has a curled-up tail, even today.

Squirrel came to the pond. The Fire Beings were right at his back. What could he do?

Then he saw small, squatty Frog, waiting and ready. Just in case. . . .

"Catch it and *jump!*" called Squirrel and threw the firebrand, which was now quite tiny.

Frog caught the firebrand, but as he jumped one of the Fire Beings grabbed his tail and pulled it off. And that's why Frog has no tail, even today.

Now when Frog jumped, he landed in the pond, and to save the flames from the water, he gulped down the tiny firebrand. He held his breath and swam over to the other side of the pond.

Then Frog saw a tree. "Catch it and *hide!*" he called and coughed up all that was left of the firebrand, just a few bright flames.

And the tree caught the fire and hid it.

The Fire Beings ran around the pond, and they looked for the fire. But it was hidden in the tree, and they didn't know how to get it out again, so they returned to their home, high on the mountaintop.

But Coyote, who is wise, knew how to get fire out of the tree. He knew how to rub two dry sticks together to make a spark that could be fed with pine needles and pine cones and grow into a fire. It was Coyote who taught the people how to do this so that they need not be cold, ever again, in wintertime. And it was Coyote who went around and gave some fire to all the other trees, so that fire lies hidden in every tree, even today.

## Reading Across Texts

What problems did you read about in *Pushing Up the Sky* and in "Catch It and Run"? How are the problems alike? How are they different?

**Writing Across Texts** Make a chart that shows the problem and solution in each of these stories.

**Author's Purpose** Why do you think the author told this story?

Night
Letters

**Comprehension**

**Skill**
Draw Conclusions

**Strategy**
Ask Questions

Skill

# Draw Conclusions

- A conclusion is a decision you reach after thinking about facts and details you read.

- You can also use what you already know to help draw a conclusion.

- Then ask yourself, "Does my conclusion make sense?"

| fact or detail | fact or detail |
|---|---|

↓ ↓

| conclusion about a character or event |
|---|

Strategy

## Strategy: Ask Questions

Good readers ask themselves questions as they read. Asking questions such as, "Why is this happening?" and "What kind of person is this character?" can help you draw conclusions.

## Write to Read

1. Read "Life on a Windowsill." Make a graphic organizer. Complete it with details and a conclusion about the kind of character Fern is.

2. Write two more questions you can ask as you read the selection. Then answer them. If necessary, draw conclusions to answer your questions.

# Life on a Windowsill

[Two potted plants are sitting on a windowsill. A human enters with a pitcher of water.]

**FERN:** It's about time! My leaves are drooping.

**IVY:** Keep your flowerpot on! The human always comes through. Mmm, the water is good!

**Strategy** This is a good place to ask a question: Why is Ivy saying, "Mmm"? What is happening?

**FERN:** My leaves are just not as green as I'd like. I want the human to raise the window shade.

[Light appears on the plants.]

**FERN:** There we go! Move over Ivy, I'm bending toward the light.

**Skill** Fern seems to complain a lot. You might draw the conclusion that Fern is a complainer. Can you draw other conclusions?

**IVY:** Please don't hog all the sunlight. There's plenty for both of us. Ahh! That sunshine feels wonderful. I feel a new leaf opening.

**FERN:** That sunshine makes me feel healthy and strong. And your new leaf is cute, cute, cute.

**IVY:** Thanks, I'm always proud of new growth.

Night Letters

## Words to Know

blade

flutter

fireflies

patch

dew

budding

notepad

**Remember**

Try the strategy. Then, if you need more help, use your glossary or a dictionary.

# Vocabulary Strategy
## for Compound Words

**Word Structure** Sometimes you may come across a long word when you are reading. Look closely at the word. If you see two smaller words, then the word probably is a compound word. You may be able to use the two smaller words to help you figure out the meaning of the compound word. For example, *sunshine* is light that shines from the sun.

**1.** Divide the compound word into its two small words.

**2.** Think of the meaning of each small word. Put the two meanings together. Does this help you understand the meaning of the compound word?

**3.** Try the meaning in the sentence. Does it make sense?

Read "Interested in Insects." Use the meanings of the smaller words in a compound word to help you understand its meaning.

# Interested in Insects

Watch a butterfly as it lands lightly on a blade of grass. Follow moths as they flutter wildly around a light. Count fireflies as they flash brightly on and off. If these things sound like fun, read on to see how you can attract these insects to your garden.

Butterflies like to sun themselves. Provide open spaces. Plant red or orange flowers in one patch and tube-shaped flowers in another. Butterflies like water, even drops of dew. Set out shallow dishes of water.

Moths are not as colorful as butterflies, but they are interesting. The hawkmoth is a large moth that can hover and fly very fast. Moths like many of the same flowers that butterflies do.

Like moths, fireflies come out at night. Turn off the outside lights, and be sure your garden has tall grass or trees. Fireflies like that.

Now when you watch budding plants and other creatures that live in the garden, you will be ready. Get out your notepad and start observing the insects.

## Words to Write

Choose two of the insects in the photographs. Write about how the two insects are alike and how they are different. Use as many words from the Words to Know list as you can.

333

# Night Letters

by Palmyra LoMonaco

illustrated by Normand Chartier

What is a night letter,
and what might it say?

Night letter time.
When supper is over
and the dishes are done,
when the clouds blush
raspberry red, and a
faraway harmonica
plays a low, sleepy song,
I know that night letter
time has come.

I put my purple notepad and pencil in my
backpack and set out to gather the letters my
backyard friends write telling me about their day.

There are zigzag lines in the dirt that I can read.

*Dear Lily,*

*My children and I picnicked on bread crumbs and sesame seeds that you dropped from your lunch.*
*Thank you.*

*Very truly yours,*
*the Ant Family*

My first night letter. I copy the words onto my pad, put it in my backpack, and walk on.

A hawkmoth rests on a crisp blade of grass.
Quietly, I bend to read what is written on its wings.

> *Dear Lily,*
> *Each evening I sip sweet nectar from the flowers,*
> *then I flutter my wings and move on.*
> *Very truly yours,*
> *the Hawkmoth*

I copy the words onto my pad, put it in my
backpack, and walk on.

The cracks in a rock in the tomato patch say,

*Dear Lily,*
*Today I touched dew and a spider's web. Now I look*
*for stars.*
*Very truly yours,*
*the Rock*

I copy the words onto my pad, put it in my
backpack, and walk on.

The fireflies switch on their flashing lights, and
if I watch without blinking, I can read their code.
*Dot-dot-dot- . . . dot-dash . . . dot-dash . . .*

*Dear Lily,*
   *Come play night sky tag. Lights on, we're here . . .*
*lights off, we're there . . . . Catch us if you can.*
   *Very truly yours,*
   *the Fireflies*

I copy the words onto my pad, put it in my
backpack, and walk on.

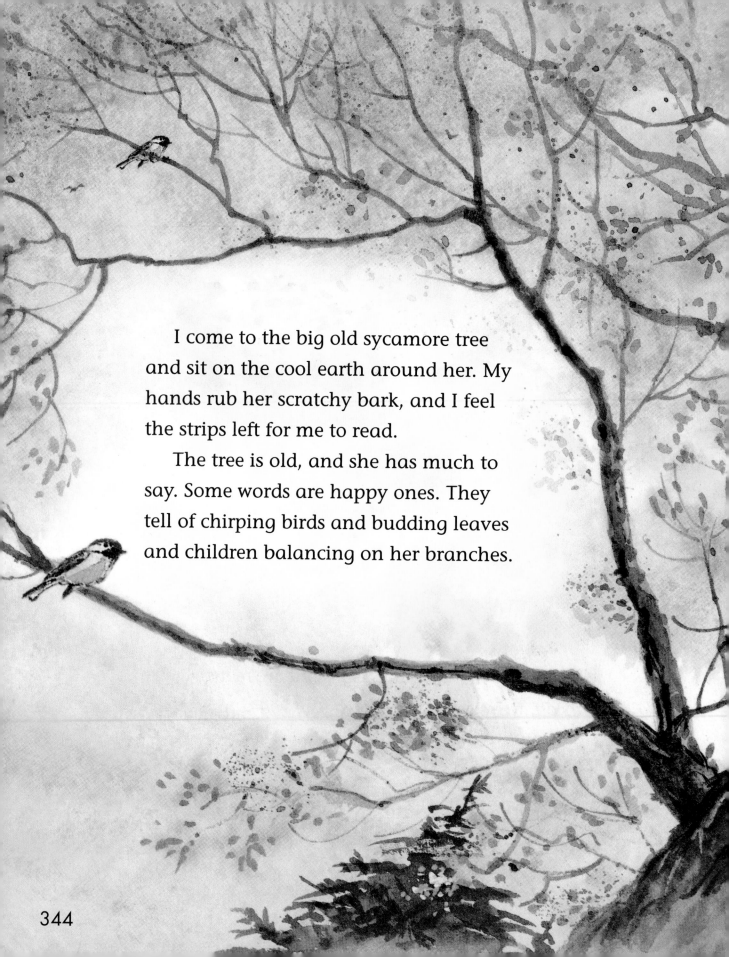

I come to the big old sycamore tree
and sit on the cool earth around her. My
hands rub her scratchy bark, and I feel
the strips left for me to read.

The tree is old, and she has much to
say. Some words are happy ones. They
tell of chirping birds and budding leaves
and children balancing on her branches.

Some words are lonely ones. They tell of birds flying south and leaves blowing away and children staying in their houses, and a time too cold for night letters.

When the faraway harmonica no longer plays its low, sleepy song, and the winds howl instead, I will tramp through the snow, over leaves long fallen, knock icicles from the tree's limbs, and wait for night letter time to return.

But right now, as the sky fades to blackberry blue, I read my last night letter.

*Dear Lily,*
*Please climb me tomorrow.*
*Very truly yours,*
*the Sycamore Tree*

I copy the words onto my pad, put it in my backpack, and walk on.

Then I turn back to the sycamore tree. "Yes," I say,
"I promise to climb you tomorrow." And I'll think about
my day and what to say to my backyard friends.

Very truly yours,
Lily

# Reader Response

**Open for Discussion** If you could suggest another night letter for this story, what would it be?

1. Authors and artists work together on a book like *Night Letters*. What do you think the author might have told the artist to help him paint the pictures? **Think Like an Author**

2. Think about what Lily does in the story. What kind of girl do you think she is? What examples from the story helped you decide? **Draw Conclusions**

3. If you could interview Lily about her book of night letters, what is one question you would like to ask her? **Ask Questions**

4. Find some compound words in the story. Use one of the two small words in each to make a new compound word. You may want to use a dictionary. Here is a sample: *hawkmoth–mothball.* **Vocabulary**

**Look Back and Write** Look back at *Night Letters*. Write the words and phrases from the selection that make it seem real.

Meet illustrator **Normand Chartier on page 420.**

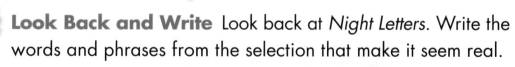

# Write Now

## Friendly Letter

**Prompt**

In *Night Letters,* Lily makes plans for the next day.

Think about a plan you have for some time in the future.

Now write a friendly letter telling a friend about your plan.

**Writing Trait**

Correct use of **conventions** (spelling, capitalization, punctuation, grammar) helps readers understand a letter.

**Student Model**

4172 Castro Street

Harrisburg, VA 22807

May 15, 2008

Dear Max,

I can't wait for our family vacation! We are going to Alaska. We will see snowy mountains and icy glaciers along the coast. I'm bringing my camera to take pictures of animals that like the cold water, such as seals. We will see tall, colorful totem poles carved by Native Americans. Our last stop will be a town where miners found gold a hundred years ago. I will send you a postcard from our 49th state!

Your friend,

Jake

**Vivid details support the main idea.**

**Writer correctly uses conventions of a friendly letter: date, greeting, and closing.**

**Proper nouns are capitalized.**

**Use the model to help you write your own friendly letter.**

351

## Genre

- Poetry is a creative expression of language.

- Often the poet's purpose is to give the reader a new way of looking at something.

- Notice that there are no capital letters or punctuation. Why do you suppose the poem is written this way?

## Link to Writing

Think of something you would say about the stars. Then write another verse for the poem.

# dear stars

written and illustrated by Takayo Noda

you are twinkling
in the moonlight
deep
  deep in the dark
  but clear sky

  I lie in a hammock
  between the trees

  I can hear insects
  and cool breezes
  bring the smell
  of mountain

    I watch you twinkling
    for the longest time
    until
      my mother calls me

    in my bed
      when I close my eyes
      you still twinkle
      inside them

## Reading Across Texts

Lily in *Night Letters* got letters from insects, a rock, and a tree. Think about what the stars might say to Lily in a letter.

**Writing Across Texts** Now write a letter to Lily from the stars.

**Visualize** What picture did you have in your head as you read the poem?

**Comprehension**

**Skill**
Generalize

**Strategy**
Answer Questions

# Generalize

- Sometimes when you read ideas about several things you can see how they are alike in some way. You can make a general statement about all of them together.

- Clue words such as *most, many, all,* or *few* signal generalizations.

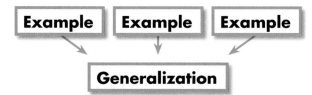

| Example | Example | Example |

**Generalization**

## Strategy: Answer Questions

Active readers ask and answer questions as they read. They know where to look for the answers. An answer might be right there in one sentence or it might be in two or more sentences. Answering questions will help you reach a generalization.

## Write to Read

**1.** Read "Songbirds of the Sea." Make a web like the one above. What generalization can you make about the sounds a beluga whale makes?

**2.** Write a one-sentence answer to the following question: What generalization does the author make about where beluga whales swim?

# Songbirds of the Sea

Beluga whales make lots of noise. They click, whistle, squeal, and grunt. They also sing. Because belugas sing so much, they are called songbirds of the sea.

Why do belugas make so much noise? Sometimes they want to talk to each other. At other times, they make noise to find things. That often means food. Beluga whales make noise for many different reasons.

Usually light from the sun does not reach ocean waters below about 325 feet. A beluga whale generally swims deeper than that. Since the whale can't see, it makes sounds. The sounds bounce off an object and back to the whale. This tells the whale where the object is. If it is a fish, the whale has found dinner.

All belugas use sound to move through ocean waters. Sound waves help a whale know where the ocean bottom is, as well as where objects are, such as rocks, boats, and icebergs.

**Strategy** Here's a question: "What generalization about beluga whales has the author made?" Look for the answer. You can find it right there in the last sentence of paragraph 2.

**Skill** Here's where you can make your own generalization. Since sunlight usually doesn't reach where a beluga whale swims, you can say that the water is dark and the whale probably can't see much.

surrounded

channel

bay

blizzards

supplies

anxiously

chipped

melody

symphony

**Remember**

Try the strategy. Then, if you need more help, use your glossary or a dictionary.

# Vocabulary Strategy
## for Unfamiliar Words

**Context Clues** Sometimes when you are reading, you come across a word you don't know. How can you figure out what the word means? Look for context clues. Context clues are the words and sentences around the word. They can help you figure out the meaning of the word.

**1.** Read the words and sentences around the word you don't know. Sometimes the author tells you what the word means.

**2.** If not, use the words and sentences to predict a meaning for the word.

**3.** Try that meaning in the sentence. Does it make sense?

As you read "Breaking the Ice," use context clues to help you understand the meanings of the vocabulary words.

# Breaking the Ice

Josh is a sailor on a Canadian icebreaker. An icebreaker is a ship with a heavy steel bow, or front, that it uses to break through ice. Sometimes a ship, surrounded on all sides by ice, becomes trapped and can't move. The icebreaker cuts a channel through the ice so that the ship can sail to safety.

Josh likes helping people. One winter, a waterfront village on a bay in the far north had been buried by blizzards. The people were running out of food and other supplies. No one could get to the village over land, so the villagers called the icebreaker for help.

The ship had to cut a path through the ice on the bay. The people were nervous and watched the ship anxiously. They chipped away the ice around the dock so that the ship could get close enough to unload the supplies. As the ship sailed away, the villagers began to sing a song. Josh did not know the melody, or tune, but he enjoyed the symphony of voices saying *thank you*.

## Words to Write

Look at the pictures in *A Symphony of Whales*. Choose a picture to write about. Try to use words from the Words to Know list.

# A Symphony of

# Whales

by Steve Schuch
illustrated by Wendell Minor

 **Genre** **Fiction** sometimes tells a story based on events that really did happen. Look for parts you think are true.

Can people communicate
with whales?

359

From the earliest time she could remember, Glashka had heard music inside her head. During the long, dark winters, blizzards sometimes lasted for days. Then her family stayed indoors, close to the small fire. Glashka heard the songs calling to her out of the darkness, beyond even the voice of the wind.

The old ones of her village said, "That is the voice of Narna, the whale. Long has she been a friend to our people. She was a friend of our grandparents' grandparents; she was a friend before we saw the boats of strange men from other lands. But it is long now

since one of us has heard her. It is a great gift you have."
And Glashka would fall asleep, wrapped in her sealskin
blanket, remembering their words.

The sea gave life to Glashka's village. The seals gave
meat and warm furs to protect against the winter cold. In
summer the people caught salmon and other fish, then
salted them to keep for the hard times to come. And from
Narna, the whale, the people received food for themselves
and their sled dogs, waterproof skins for their parkas and
boots, and oil for their lamps in the long winter darkness.

One year the snows came early. For three days a
blizzard bore down on the village. When it finally stopped,
Glashka's family needed supplies from the next village.
Glashka asked if she might help drive the sled dogs. "It is
not so easy to drive the sled," her parents said. "The dogs
will know if you are uncertain of the way. But you will
know the way home. Perhaps on the way back, you may
try. Now go to sleep."

That night in her dreams, Glashka drove the dogsled. But the dogs did not follow her commands. Instead they led her to open water surrounded by ice. Glashka heard the singing of Narna, louder than she had ever heard it before. She awoke in the darkness of her sealskins, wondering what the dream had meant.

The morning was clear and cold as the family set out. The dogs made good time to the neighboring village. Before starting back, Glashka's parents packed the supplies into the sled. Glashka checked the dogs' feet for cuts. She rubbed their ears and necks. Glashka's parents gave her the reins. "We'll follow behind you. If your heart

and words are clear, the dogs will listen and take you where you wish to go."

They set off. Across the ice, snow swirled as the wind began to pick up. Suddenly the sled dogs broke from the trail, yelping and twitching their ears. "What is it?" Glashka's parents shouted.

"I think they hear something," Glashka called back.

The sled dogs pulled harder. Their keen ears could pick up high-pitched notes that most humans couldn't hear. But Glashka, if she turned just right, could make out the eerie moans and whistles that grew louder until even her parents could hear them.

The dogs stopped short. They were right at the edge of a great bay of open water, surrounded on all sides by ice and snow.

Everywhere Glashka looked, the water seemed to be heaving and boiling, choked with white whales. Her father came up beside her. "Beluga whales," he said softly.

Glashka stared. "There must be more than a thousand of them."

The cries of the whales rose and fell on the wind as they swam slowly about. The dogs whined and pawed anxiously at the ice. "Let's hurry to the village," cried Glashka. "We'll get help!"

Glashka's father, though, knew there was no help. "They must have been trapped when they came here last fall looking for food," he said quietly. "There's nothing we can do to free them. When the last of the water freezes over, the whales will die."

But Glashka's mother remembered that an icebreaker, several winters ago, had rescued a Russian freighter trapped in the sea ice. "Could we call on the emergency radio? Maybe an icebreaker can clear a channel for the whales," she said.

Glashka and her parents raced back to their village. They gathered everyone together and told them what had happened. Glashka's father got on the emergency radio and put out a distress call. "Beluga whales, maybe thousands of them, trapped. We need an icebreaker. Can anyone hear me?"

Far out at sea, a great Russian icebreaker named the *Moskva* picked up the faint signal. "We read you," the captain radioed back. "We're on our way, but it may take us several weeks to reach you. Can you keep the whales alive until then?"

Some of the people from Glashka's village started setting up a base camp near the whales. Others set out by dogsled to alert the surrounding settlements.

Everyone came—young and old, parents, grandparents, and children. Day after day they chipped back the edges of the ice, trying to make more room for the whales to come up to breathe. "Look," said Glashka's grandmother. "See how the whales are taking turns, how they give the younger ones extra time for air."

As Glashka took her turn chipping back the ice, the song of Narna filled her ears again. She sang to the whales while she worked, trying to let them know help was on the way. Each day, Glashka looked anxiously for a ship. But each day, a little more water turned to ice. Each day, the whales got weaker from hunger.

Glashka knew how it felt to be hungry. The year before, her village had caught barely enough fish to make it through to spring. Sometimes the memory still gnawed at her. Even so, she gave the whales part of the fish from her lunch. The other villagers noticed and began to feed some of their own winter fish to the whales too.

One morning Glashka awoke to the sounds of excited voices and barking dogs. The icebreaker had broken through the main channel during the night. "Hurry,

Glashka," her parents called. Glashka pulled on her boots and parka and ran down the path to the water.

Everyone was gathered. Off to one side, the old ones stood, watching. They beckoned Glashka to join them. "Now," they said, "let us see what the whales will do."

The whales crowded together in fear, keeping as far from the icebreaker as possible. On board the ship, the captain gave orders. He hoped the whales would see the pathway cleared through the ice and follow the ship to safety. The icebreaker slowly turned around and faced back out to sea.

But the whales wouldn't follow the ship. "They may be afraid of the noise of our engines," the captain radioed to shore. "I've heard that trapped whales will sometimes follow the singing of other whales. We'll try playing a recording of whale songs."

Glashka felt a shiver down her back. "Narna's songs," she whispered to the sled dogs. "They're going to play Narna's songs."

Then the songs of the whales echoed over the water—deep moans and high whistling calls, ancient sounds from another world.

But the whales would not go near the ship. Again and again, the captain inched the giant icebreaker closer to the whales, then back toward the sea. But the whales stayed as far away as they could.

"It's no use," the captain radioed in despair. "And we can't stay beyond tomorrow. Already the channel is starting to refreeze!"

Glashka was near tears as she asked the old ones what could be done now. "Wait," they said. "Let us see what tomorrow brings."

That night the song of Narna came to Glashka again. Only this time it was different. She heard the music and voices of whales, but she heard other music too . . . melodies she'd never before. . . . While it was still dark, Glashka woke her parents. "I've heard Narna again," she said. "And I've heard other music too!"

"You have to tell the old ones," Glashka's parents said.

The old ones of the village listened carefully as Glashka told them what she had heard. "So, it is other music Narna is asking for," they said thoughtfully. "Long is the time, but once, it is said, humans and whales made music together. Perhaps the time has come again. Let us speak with the captain!"

Quickly Glashka and the old ones radioed the ship. "Have you any other music, people music, to play for the whales?" they asked. The captain said he would see what his crew could find.

First, they tried playing rock and roll. The electric guitars and drums boomed, but the whales would not follow the ship.

Next, the crew tried Russian folk music. It was softer, with many voices singing together. The whales swam a little closer, but still they would not follow the ship.

On shore, Glashka ran back to the radio transmitter. She had to talk with the captain. "I *know* there's other music that will work. Please keep trying!" she told him.

The crew found some classical music. First the sweet sounds of violins and violas, next the deeper notes of the cellos and, deepest of all, the string basses . . . and way up high, a solo violin. . . .

Everyone fell silent as the melody carried over the water. The whales grew quiet, too, listening.

A few whales started to sing back to the ship and to each other. Gradually more whales joined in.

Then . . . they began to swim toward the ship!

Cautiously the captain started the huge engines and headed slowly out to sea. One whale followed, then another, then a few more. Soon all the whales were following the ship through the narrow channel, past the broken chunks of ice, back to the safety of the open ocean.

On shore, people laughed and cried and hugged each other. The sled dogs jumped up and barked, trying to lick the noses and faces of anyone they could reach. Glashka buried her wet face in the fur of the dogs' necks. "Such good, good dogs," she told them over and over. "Such good dogs. Now the whales are going home!"

On board the ship, the captain and his crew raised every flag. The music played as the captain radioed to say the whales were safe. He and his crew were finally going home too.

Glashka and her family looked out to sea. They waved to the icebreaker and the disappearing whales. "And do you hear Narna singing now?" her grandmother asked.

"Yes," Glashka said, "but it isn't just Narna I hear now. It's something bigger than that . . . something like a whole symphony of whales!"

# Reader Response

**Open for Discussion** What did you think was the most exciting part of the story? Why was that part exciting?

1. The author begins his story with Glashka hearing music inside her head. How does that beginning get you ready for the rest of the story? **Think Like an Author**

2. Think about the lives of the villagers and the lives of the whales. What does that say about how people and nature are connected? **Generalize**

3. At the end of the story, Glashka tells the sled dogs that they are good dogs. Why does she believe they are good dogs? **Answer Questions**

4. The list words *symphony* and *melody* are related to music. What other words from the story could you include in that group? **Vocabulary**

**Look Back and Write** The old ones talk about "other music." What is the "other music," and why is it important? Use story details to support your answer.

**Meet author Steve Schuch on page 410 and illustrator Wendell Minor on page 421.**

# Write Now

## News Story

**Prompt**

*A Symphony of Whales* describes an event in a small village that could be the subject of a real-life news story.

Think about an event that took place in your town or neighborhood.

Now write a news story about that event that answers the *5 Ws* and *How.*

**Writing Trait**

Using different kinds and lengths of **sentences** helps make a news story clear and interesting.

Questions *who, what, when, where, why,* and *how* are answered at beginning of news story.

Different kinds and lengths of <u>sentences</u> make writing flow.

**Student Model**

Last week, something unusual happened in Cherrydale. A Hollywood crew came to shoot Town Square, a movie about a small town in the 1800s. They thought the buildings on Main Street had just the right old-fashioned look. The movie takes place in winter, so the snowy street was perfect. About 100 local men, women, and children performed as extras. They dressed in 19th-century costumes and walked or rode horses up and down Main Street. Are you excited about seeing Cherrydale 100 years ago? Then go see the movie next summer.

**Use the model to help you write your own news story.**

## Expository Nonfiction

### Genre

- An expository nonfiction article gives facts.

- Nonfiction articles often include photos or illustrations.

### Text Features

- The author uses dialogue from the expert, Joe, to tell facts.

- Captions give more information. You can read the captions after you finish reading the article.

### Link to Science

Use the Internet or other references to find out more about the whale songs. Write a short report to share with your classmates.

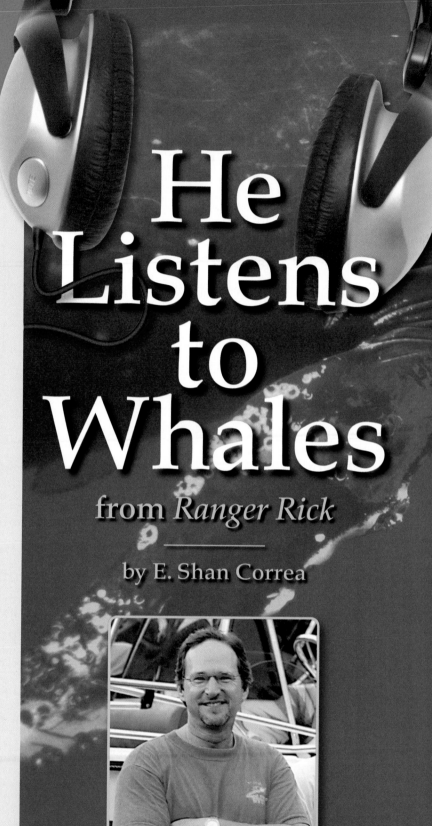

# He Listens to Whales

from *Ranger Rick*

by E. Shan Correa

Joe Mobley, marine biologist

*Humpback whales chatter and call to each other—and they sing songs for hours. What does all this humpback "hollering" mean? Here's one scientist who's trying to find out.*

Joe Mobley lives near the island of Maui in Hawaii. (*Maui* rhymes with "*zowie.*") It's the perfect place for a scientist who studies how humpback whales behave. The whales hang out near Maui all winter long.

Joe has lots of questions about these huge mammals.

How do they know where to go when they travel through the ocean? How do they find each other? How do groups stay together? Joe thinks clues to these mysteries are held in the sounds that these whales make. To collect clues, he listens to the humpbacks.

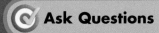 **Ask Questions**   What questions did you have as you read?

377

## Whale Chatter

"Humpbacks make three main types of sounds," Joe explains. "Both the males and the females call loudly when they're hungry or eating. Males 'talk' when they're hanging out in groups. And males sing during mating time."

Joe first heard the whales' feeding calls from a tape that another scientist had made. The whales were feeding in their summer home off the coast of Alaska. All were scooping up small fish and shrimplike krill with their enormous mouths. And they seemed to call to each other while they ate. "You can imagine how noisy they were!" Joe says with a laugh. "They eat all the time during the summer," he continues, "but they almost never eat during the winter."

To listen to whales in winter, Joe doesn't have to go far. He just heads to their winter home in the ocean around Maui. That's when he hears the second kind of whale sound, which he calls "talking."

Joe explains what the sounds may mean: "Whales hang out in groups called *pods.* While they're in pods, the male whales make strange clicks, creaks, roars, and whines. Some of them seem to be signaling to females, as if they were saying, 'Hey, I'm over here!' Or they might be saying to other males, 'This is my mate, so stay away.' So far, no one has heard females or young whales 'talking' in this way."

This scientist is listening for whale calls.

These scientists are recording humpback whale songs.

## Long Songs

Whale songs are the third kind of sound that Joe studies. You may have heard them on records. Some parts of a whale's song sound sad, like children crying. Some parts are high squeaks. And some rumble like thunder.

"These songs are beautiful, but *loud!*" Joe says. "They're much louder than any other animal sound, louder even than rock music. Our boat shakes when a singing whale is close by."

A humpback's song has parts that are repeated over and over. One song can last 30 minutes.

Then the whale might repeat the whole song. Sometimes a humpback sings for more than 20 hours without stopping!

## Reading Across Texts

You have read *A Symphony of Whales* about beluga whales and "He Listens to Whales" about humpback whales. What do the two kinds of whales have in common?

**Writing Across Texts** Create a Venn diagram to compare and contrast the two.

**Generalize** In general, what can you say about whale songs?

379

**Comprehension**

**Skill**
Compare
and Contrast

**Strategy**
Monitor
and Fix Up

Skill

# Compare and Contrast

- When you compare and contrast, you tell how two or more things are alike and different.

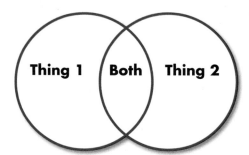

Thing 1 • Both • Thing 2

Strategy

## Strategy: Monitor and Fix Up

Active readers check their understanding as they read. Reading more slowly helps you notice details, key words, or other clues the author uses in comparing and contrasting.

# Write to Read

**1.** Make a diagram like the one above. Write "Paricutín" in one circle and "Other Volcanoes" in the other. As you read "From Cornfield to Volcano," compare and contrast by writing details in the diagram.

**2.** Use your graphic organizer to write a paragraph comparing Paricutín with other volcanoes. If you missed some details, go back and read the article more slowly.

# From Cornfield to Volcano

Although some volcanoes seem silent, they may still erupt one day. Others are dead and will not erupt again. Most volcanoes grow into mountains over thousands of years. Yet one, called Paricutín, erupted from flat land and grew quickly.

One day in 1943, a Mexican farmer noticed a new crack in his field. Then he felt the earth shake. What happened next was really a surprise. The farmer saw the ground lift up about fifteen feet out of the crack! As in eruptions of other volcanoes, ash began pouring out, and the air smelled like rotten eggs.

By the next morning, the new volcano had grown thirty feet. At the end of the week, the volcano was 450 feet high. In two months, Paricutín grew 1,000 feet!

Like other volcanoes, Paricutín damaged farms and towns. Its latest eruption was in 1952, nine years after its first.

**1** **Skill** Here is a detail that tells one way Paricutín is different from most volcanoes.

**2** **Strategy** This might be confusing. If you are having trouble understanding, slow down. A comparison between Paricutín and other volcanoes is coming up.

## Words to Know

beneath

earthquakes

volcanoes

fireworks

force

trembles

chimney

buried

# Vocabulary Strategy
## for Unfamiliar Words

**Dictionary** You can use a dictionary to find the meaning of an unfamiliar word. A dictionary gives words and their meanings, as well as other information about the words. The words in a dictionary are listed in alphabetical order.

**1.** Look at the first letter in the word.

**2.** Turn in the dictionary to the section for that letter.

**3.** Use the guide words at the top of the pages to find the page that has the word.

**4.** Read the entry for the word. If the word has more than one meaning, decide which meaning you think fits in the sentence.

**5.** Try that meaning to see if it makes sense.

Read "The Active Earth." Use a dictionary to find the meanings of the vocabulary words.

# The ACTIVE Earth

We think of Earth as rock solid. Rock, maybe; solid, not exactly. Far beneath our feet, powerful forces are always at work. Earthquakes shake the ground. Volcanoes erupt sending fireworks into the sky. Why?

The top layer of Earth, its crust, is composed of large pieces called plates. When two of these plates bump, the force can break rocks. When that occurs, the ground trembles and shakes. That's an earthquake.

Below the crust it is so hot that rocks melt. This melted rock, called *magma,* moves up toward the crust. If there is a crack in the crust, the magma rises through the crack, like smoke through a chimney. Then the magma flows out onto the surface as red, glowing lava. Huge areas may be buried. That's a volcano.

So, the next time you take a walk, think about what is going on far, far below your feet.

## Words to Write

Look at this volcano. Write about what you see. Use words that will help others "see" what you see. Use words from the Words to Know list.

**Genre**

**Expository nonfiction** gives facts and information.
Look for facts about volcanoes as you read.

# Volcanoes

## NATURE'S INCREDIBLE FIREWORKS

by David L. Harrison

Do we know when volcanoes will erupt?

Earth is never still. Every day somewhere it trembles and quivers. Every day somewhere volcanoes erupt. From far off they look like beautiful fireworks.

But up close, a volcano is no fun. What looks like sparks are fiery blobs of melted rock called *lava*.

Gases and geysers of scalding hot steam, ground-up rocks, and gritty ashes blast into the air and turn the sky dark.

If too much gas is trapped inside, part of the mountain may blow off, hurling rocks heavier than elephants for miles. Some explosions cause floods, mud slides, and avalanches that roar downhill, destroying everything in their path.

But not all volcanoes explode. If enough gas escapes first, red rivers of lava flow out through the cracks and crevices.

Some kinds of lava ooze and slide slowly. Others stream down the mountain as quickly as cars in city traffic.

How do rocks get so hot that they melt? What causes volcanoes? The answers lie deep beneath our feet in the four parts of the earth—the crust, the mantle, the outer core, and the inner core.

The crust, where we live, is covered by land and oceans. In places under the seas the crust is only three miles deep. It may be forty-three miles thick beneath the mountains.

Below the crust, the mantle stretches down 1,800 miles. Rocks there melt to a gooey paste or tar called *magma*.

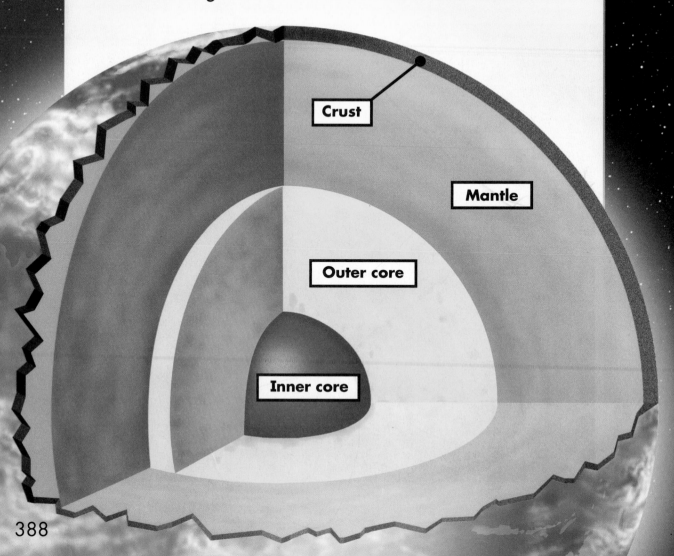

Crust

Mantle

Outer core

Inner core

The core is a huge ball more than 2,100 miles to its center. It is mostly iron so hot that the outer core is liquid. But the inner core is solid. Pressure there is so great it keeps the iron from melting.

The crust is not one piece like a coconut shell. It is several large pieces called *plates* that cover the planet like a giant jigsaw puzzle.

The plates rest on the mantle below. They are moving, but they move slowly. Some take years to creep inches.

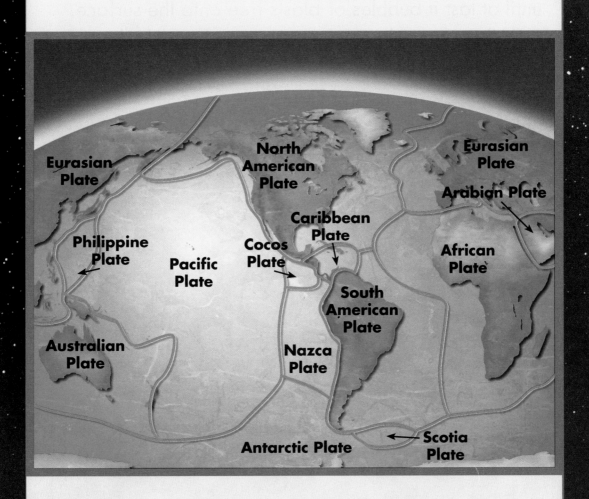

Where two plates meet, the force is so great that rocks bend or even break. That sends tremors called *earthquakes* through the ground. Most earthquakes are small and do no harm.

But sometimes part of a plate gets caught, and when it finally snaps back, the ground shudders hard and causes great damage. In 1906, a major earthquake destroyed much of San Francisco, California.

Most magma moves toward the crust where it cools and sinks again. But some magma breaks through weak spots by rising through cracks like chimney flues until at last it bubbles or blasts free onto the surface.

Where two plates meet, the mantle grows hotter, and volcanoes form near the edges. Many big volcanoes form in the ocean. We don't see them unless they rise above the water as islands.

The state of Hawaii is a group of volcanoes. Some stand 30,000 feet above the ocean floor. That is more than five and one-half miles high.

Around the Pacific Ocean, so many plates collide with one another that many of the world's greatest eruptions have happened there. We call it the Ring of Fire.

In the United States, Mount St. Helens erupted in 1980 with such force that part of the mountain exploded.

One of the most famous volcanoes in history is Mount Vesuvius in Italy. When it erupted in A.D. 79 it buried the cities of Pompeii and Herculaneum under ash, mud, and lava.

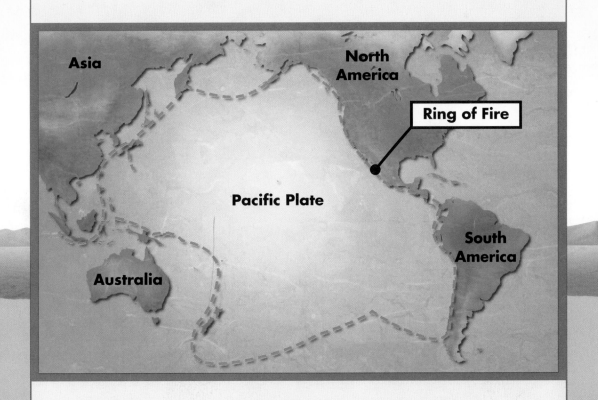

Asia

North America

Ring of Fire

Pacific Plate

South America

Australia

Over thousands of years, a volcano may erupt again and again. Between eruptions, it may sleep in silence for long periods.

After each eruption, lava cools into rock, and ash settles to the ground. Layers of lava and ash slowly build the volcano until it becomes a tall mountain.

As new magma pushes against the surface, rocks move and the ground shakes. These earthquakes help us know the volcano may be getting ready to erupt.

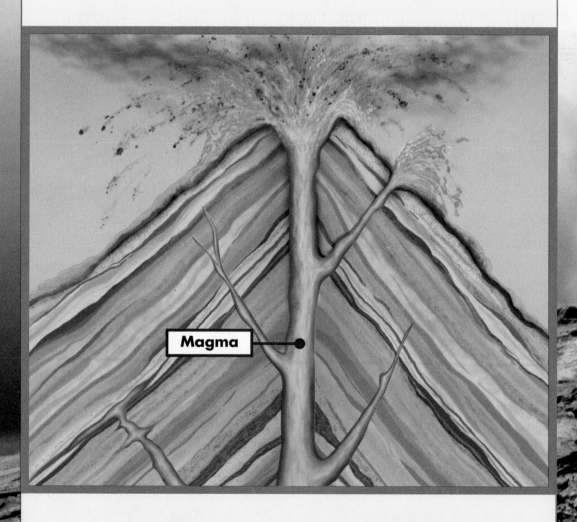

Magma

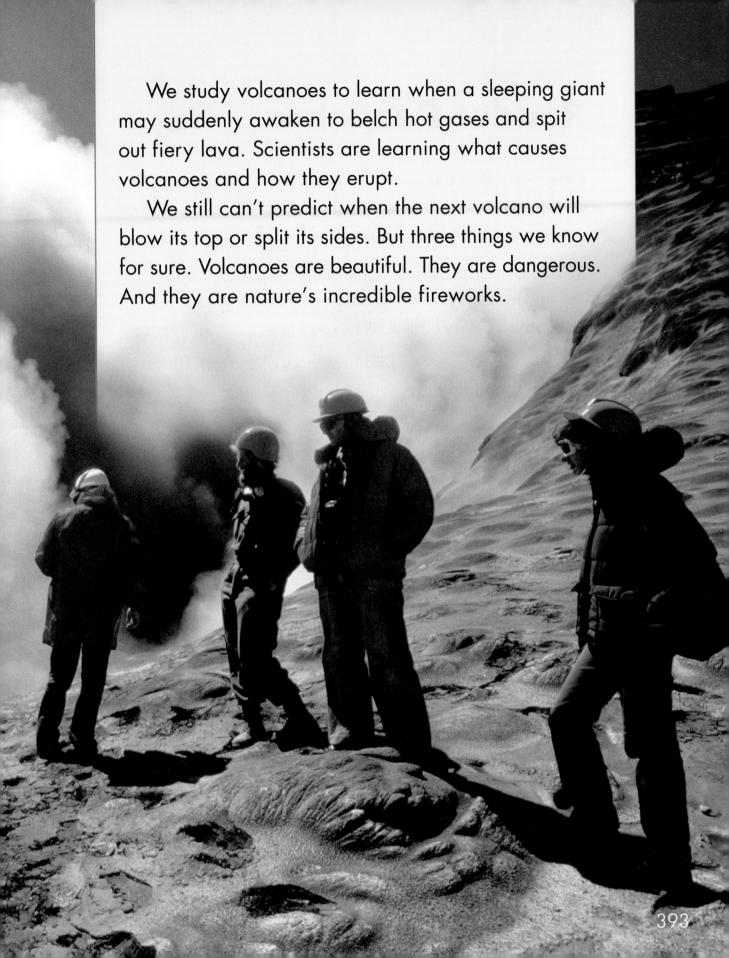

We study volcanoes to learn when a sleeping giant may suddenly awaken to belch hot gases and spit out fiery lava. Scientists are learning what causes volcanoes and how they erupt.

We still can't predict when the next volcano will blow its top or split its sides. But three things we know for sure. Volcanoes are beautiful. They are dangerous. And they are nature's incredible fireworks.

# Reader Response

**Open for Discussion** Your friend says, "I'm glad I live on this quiet, solid Earth." After reading this article, what can you tell your friend about this Earth?

1. The author provides many interesting facts about volcanoes. What was the most interesting fact you learned? Why? **Think Like an Author**

2. How are volcanoes and fireworks alike from far off? How are they different up close? **Compare and Contrast**

3. How did you make sure that you understood the information about volcanoes as you read this selection? **Monitor and Fix Up**

4. You are a newspaper reporter. Tell your readers what it is like to watch a volcano erupt. Use words from the Words to Know list to describe the event. **Vocabulary**

**Look Back and Write** Look back at pages 386–387. What can happen when a volcano erupts? Use details from the selection in your answer.

**Meet author David Harrison on page 416.**

394

# Write Now

## Compare/Contrast Paragraph

### Prompt

*Volcanoes* describes natural events, such as volcanoes and earthquakes.

Think about two natural events you have seen or read about.

Now write a paragraph that compares and contrasts these two natural events.

### Writing Trait

**Word choice** can show comparisons and contrasts. Words such as *also, both, but,* and *however* show likenesses and differences.

**Student Model**

**First sentence tells what two natural events are being compared.**

**Word choice** includes words that signal likenesses and differences.

**Writer begins and ends with likenesses.**

Tornadoes and hurricanes are both storms. However, they are different kinds of storms, and they usually happen in different places. A tornado is a funnel-shaped cloud with very high winds. Tornadoes often occur in the central United States. A hurricane starts over the ocean. Like a tornado, it has very high winds, but it also brings lots of rain and high waves. Hurricanes usually hit the Atlantic coast or the Gulf coast. Both tornadoes and hurricanes are dangerous.

**Use the model to help you write your own compare/contrast paragraph.**

## Search Engines

### Genre

- A search engine helps you find Web sites on the Internet.

- Use *keywords* to find a Web site on your topic.

### Text Features

- The search engine window is where you type in a keyword.

- Click on the SEARCH button to see the results listed below the search window.

- Each item on the list is a link to a Web site that contains your keyword.

### Link to Science

Use the library or the Internet to find out about another natural disaster such as a *tsunami*. Draw a diagram to explain it.

# Natural Disasters

People usually get along with nature just fine. Sometimes, though, nature can cause great harm to people, animals, and other wildlife. Such events are called natural disasters. You want to learn more about them.

For more practice

**Take It** to the Net

PearsonSuccessNet.com

You type the keywords *natural disasters* into a search engine and click SEARCH. If you search using a phrase, it helps to put the phrase in quotation marks.

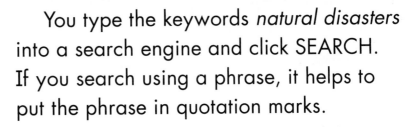

File   Edit   View   Favorites

http://www.url.here

"natural disasters"                               Search

The search engine you choose might offer a list of Web sites about natural disasters. You might find results such as the following.

File   Edit   View   Fav

"natural disasters"                    Search

1. Survivors of **Natural Disasters.** Every year, millions of Americans are affected by natural disasters. Survivors face the danger of death or physical injury and the loss of everything they own.

2. **Natural Disasters.** A Bibliography. This bibliography lists books about natural disasters.

3. **Natural Disasters.** ▷ Natural disasters are extreme, sudden events caused by nature that injure people and damage property. Earthquakes, windstorms, floods, and disease all strike anywhere on earth, often without warning.

The third link to Natural Disasters may seem interesting to you. You click on it.

✅ **Monitor and Fix Up**   Are you confused? Reread if you need to.

When you click on the link, you might see a computer screen such as this:

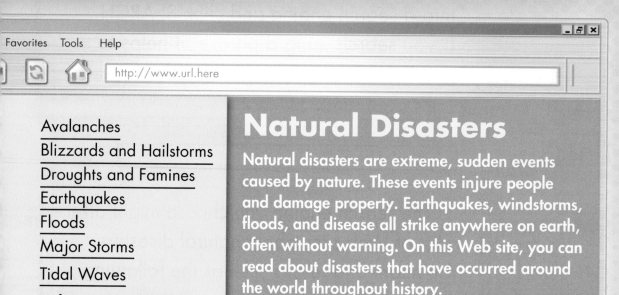

Favorites   Tools   Help

http://www.url.here

Avalanches
Blizzards and Hailstorms
Droughts and Famines
Earthquakes
Floods
Major Storms
Tidal Waves
**Volcanic Eruptions**

# Natural Disasters

Natural disasters are extreme, sudden events caused by nature. These events injure people and damage property. Earthquakes, windstorms, floods, and disease all strike anywhere on earth, often without warning. On this Web site, you can read about disasters that have occurred around the world throughout history.

If you click on Volcanic Eruptions, this is what you get.

# Volcanic Eruptions

On August 26, 1883, the island volcano of Krakatoa in Indonesia exploded. The eruption was one of the worst natural disasters in recorded history. The effects were experienced all over the world.

**Above: Krakatoa prior to the eruption.**

**Below: Krakatoa after the eruption.**

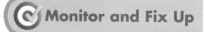 **Monitor and Fix Up**   Read more slowly if you don't understand.

Fine ashes from the Krakatoa eruption were carried by winds as far away as New York City. That was half the world away. The explosion was heard more than 3,000 miles away. Volcanic dust blew into the upper air affecting Earth's weather for several years.

A series of large waves generated by the main explosion killed more than 36,000 people. Some of these waves were nearly 40 meters (more than 120 feet) tall. These large waves were observed as far away as the English Channel.

1883 cover of the *London News* newspaper.

The island of Krakatoa as it looks today.

## Reading Across Texts

Both selections you have read tell how powerful volcanoes can be. Think about what you learned from the print selection and the Internet selection.

**Writing Across Texts** Write a paragraph about what you learned from each selection.

# Cloud Dragons

**by Pat Mora**

What do you see
in the clouds so high?
What do you see in the sky?

Oh, I see dragons
that curl their tails
as they go slithering by.

What do you see
in the clouds so high?
What do you see? Tell me, do.

Oh, I see *caballitos*
that race the wind
high in the shimmering blue.

# LEMON MOON

**by Beverly McLoughland**

On a hot and thirsty summer night,
The moon's a wedge of lemon light
Sitting low among the trees,
Close enough for you to squeeze
And make a moonade, icy-sweet,
To cool your summer-dusty heat.

# Hurt No Living Thing

**by Christina Rossetti**

Hurt no living thing;
 Ladybird, nor butterfly,
 Nor moth with dusty wing,
Nor cricket chirping cheerily,
Nor grasshopper so light of leap,
 Nor dancing gnat, nor beetle fat,
 Nor harmless worms that creep.

401

# Springtime

**by Nikki Giovanni**

in springtime the violets
grow in the sidewalk cracks
and the ants play furiously
at my gym-shoed toes
carrying off a half-eaten peanut
butter sandwich i had at lunch
and sometimes i crumble
my extra graham crackers
and on the rainy days i take off
my yellow space hat and splash
all the puddles on Pendry Street and not one
cold can catch me

# Laughing Boy

## by Richard Wright

In the falling snow
A laughing boy holds out his palms
Until they are white.

## Dear Person

In *Night Letters* you read what different parts of nature might say if they could write a letter to a human. Choose a plant, an animal, or another part of nature around you. Make notes with details about what it might hear, smell, taste, feel, see, and say. Then use your notes to write a letter from that animal, plant, or part of nature.

# How are people and nature connected?

## Making Connections

Pick out the most important character in each selection from this unit. Then tell the part of nature that the character connects to and how the two are connected. Continue a chart like the one below.

| Character | Part of nature | How they are connected |
|-----------|----------------|------------------------|
| Glashka | Whales | Glashka hears the whale voices. |
| | | |

## Nature Web

In this unit, you learned how people and parts of nature connect to one another. In a group, assign an element of nature to each person. Sit in a circle. The first person holds a ball of yarn and tells how one other person in the circle is important to the element of nature he/she represents. Then the first person passes the ball of yarn to the person he/she chose, but still holds the end of the yarn. Take turns passing the ball of yarn and telling ways that the elements of nature are connected.

# Genre Study

What do you like to read? Fairy tales? Biography? Mystery? Select a favorite genre and do a study. For example, a genre study of realistic fiction might compare *My Rows and Piles of Coins* with *The Gardener*.

**Try It**

- Define the genre.
- Set up a chart with special features of the genre.
- Read two or more examples of the genre.
- Compare selections and complete the chart.

**Realistic fiction** is a made-up story that could really happen.

| Selection | Characters | Setting | Problem/Solution |
|---|---|---|---|
| *My Rows and Piles of Coins* by Tololwa M. Mollel | Saruni<br>his mother, Yeyo<br>his father, Murete | African village | Saruni can't afford a bike to help on market day. Saruni uses his father's bike. |
| *The Gardener* by Sarah Stewart | Lydia Grace<br>Grandma<br>Uncle Jim<br>Emma | Big city during hard times | Lydia Grace is homesick. She makes friends and plants a garden. |

A chart for historical fiction might have headings such as these: Title, Topic, Historical Facts, and Fictional Elements.

# Author Study

Do you have a favorite selection? Make a note of the author's name and look for books by that author. You will probably enjoy other works by him or her.

**Try It**

- Find three or four works by one author.
- Read the book jackets or use the Internet to learn about the author's life to see what may have influenced his or her writing.
- Read the author's works.
- Compare topics, genres, and so on.
- Tell which work is your favorite and why.

Read this author study of David Harrison.

### David Harrison

David Harrison has always been interested in nature. "I began collecting bits of nature as a third grader." It started with insects, but it grew into "just about anything I could carry home and convince my mother to let me keep in my room." Mr. Harrison has written many books for young people, including poetry and nonfiction about the Earth. My favorite books are in his _Earthworks_ series.

# Meet Authors of Realistic Fiction

## Eve Bunting
**The author of *A Day's Work*, p. 178 of Vol. 1**

Eve Bunting grew up in Ireland. When she was seven years old, she went to a boarding school. "Perhaps it was there in the telling of tall tales after 'lights out,' that I got my first taste of storytelling. It was certainly there that I developed my lifelong love of books and reading." She and her family moved to the United States in 1958. "We had it pretty hard at the beginning," Ms. Bunting says. *A Day's Work* shows her understanding of some of the difficulties that immigrants face. Some of Ms. Bunting's books are happy and fun. But she often writes about serious topics such as homelessness, war, and poverty. **Other books: *Dreaming of America* and *Butterfly House***

## Claire Hartfield
**The author of *Me and Uncle Romie*, p. 248 of Vol. 2**

Claire Hartfield likes to dance. She began taking dance lessons when she was five. Dance was always her way of telling stories. But in *Me and Uncle Romie*, Claire Hartfield wanted to show how an artist can use art to tell stories. Although *Me and Uncle Romie* is fiction, it is based on the life of collage artist Romare Bearden. Today, Ms. Hartfield is a lawyer in Chicago. **Other books about art: *Loo-Loo, Boo and Art You Can Do* and *Recycled Crafts Box***

## Tololwa Mollel
**The author of *My Rows and Piles of Coins*, p. 120 of Vol. 1**

Tololwa Mollel grew up in a small village in Tanzania, Africa. Mr. Mollel often went to the market with his grandmother. "It was the only time I got any money!" he says. "But the boy in the story is smarter than I was because he saved his money." **Other books: *The Orphan Boy* and *Kele's Secret***

## Frances Park and Ginger Park
**The authors of *Good-Bye, 382 Shin Dang Dong*, p. 198 of Vol. 2**

Frances and Ginger Park are sisters. They often work as a team to create a book. Although their parents came from Korea, Frances and Ginger Park were born near Washington, D.C. The sisters own a chocolate shop. People often stop by to talk about their books. "We pack up truffles, and then talk books," says Frances. **Other books: *Where on Earth Is My Bagel?* and *My Freedom Trip***

## Susan L. Roth
**The author/illustrator of *Happy Birthday Mr. Kang*, p. 308 of Vol. 2**

Susan L. Roth got the idea for *Happy Birthday Mr. Kang* from a newspaper story about a group of Chinese men who brought their *hua mei* to a park each Sunday. Ms. Roth went to the park to see. "It was very noisy," she said. "The birds were clearly communicating with each other." **Other books: *The Biggest Frog in Australia* and *How Thunder and Lightning Came to Be***

# Meet Authors of Realistic Fiction

## Steve Schuch

**The author of *A Symphony of Whales*, p. 358 of Vol. 1**

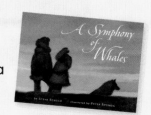

Steve Schuch first became interested in whales when a scientist who was also a musician came to his college. The musician played his cello along with recordings of whale songs. "That evening forever changed how I heard music and thought about whales," says Mr. Schuch.

## Sarah Stewart

**The author of *The Gardener*, p. 284 of Vol. 1**

As a child, Sarah Stewart's favorite places were the library and her grandmother's garden. She loved quiet places where she could think and dream. At the library she would daydream with a book. "In my grandmother's garden, I could dig in the earth or cut a bouquet or simply lie down between the rows and listen to the silence." **Other books: *The Library* and *The Journey***

## Chieri Uegaki

**The author of *Suki's Kimono*, p. 150 of Vol. 2**

Chieri Uegaki began writing at the age of seven when she published a family newspaper. Ms. Uegaki says about her writing: "It makes me very happy to think that something I've written could touch someone and perhaps even become someone's favorite." Ms. Uegaki based *Suki's Kimono* on her relationship with her Japanese grandmother. **Other books about children like Suki: *First Day, Hooray!* and *It's Back to School We Go!***

## Judith Viorst

**The author of *Alexander, Who Used to Be Rich Last Sunday*, p. 68 of Vol. 1**

Judith Viorst based the character of Alexander on the youngest of her three children. "Four of the books I've written for children, I consciously sat down and wrote because one child or another of mine had a problem." She hoped her books would help her sons "laugh at their own problems." **Other books: *Alexander and the Terrible, Horrible, No Good, Very Bad Day* and *Super-Completely and Totally the Messiest***

## Natasha Wing

**The author of *Jalapeño Bagels*, p. 224 of Vol. 2**

Natasha Wing lives in northern California, where she often buys jalapeño bagels at a bakery in town. The bakery, called Los Bagels Bakery and Café, gave Ms. Wing the idea for this story. Los Bagels offers many tasty snacks, such as Mexican hot chocolate, pumpkin turnovers, and bagels topped with jalapeño jelly.

**Another book: *The Night Before Summer Vacation***

## Ginger Howard

### The author of *William's House*, p. 254 of Vol. 1

Ginger Howard got the idea to write *William's House* while doing research for another book. She read about the houses that were built in early America. She learned that it took time for people to learn what kinds of houses were comfortable in a New England climate. "The early American settlers were brave to leave the comfort of their homes for an unknown land. The ones who found the most happiness made goals and were willing to change." **Other books about home building:** *I Have Heard of a Land* and *Nothing Here But Trees*

## Sonia Levitin

### The author of *Boom Town*, p. 16 of Vol. 1

Some of Sonia Levitin's favorite things as a child were animals, climbing trees, and reading. When she was eleven, she wrote a letter to her favorite author, Laura Ingalls Wilder. "I told her I wanted to become an author too." It was the first time she had told anyone her dream. Amazingly, she received a reply. The letter remains one of her greatest treasures. It took a while, but Ms. Levitin finally did achieve her goal. She has now written over forty award-winning books. **Other books:** *Nine for California* and *Taking Charge*

## Joseph Bruchac

**The author of *Pushing Up the Sky*, p. 308 of Vol. 1**

Joseph Bruchac grew up in a small town in the mountains in New York. As a young boy he loved reading and nature. Often he would go off to read books deep in the forest. Some Native American tribes have stories to explain just about every part of nature. "Those stories tell us so much about nature and are a lot easier to remember than a bunch of facts." Bruchac has traveled all over America listening to stories of different Indian tribes. He has always been a very careful listener. "The first thing I always tell young people is to listen. A good storyteller is a good listener first." **Other books: *The Boy Who Lived with the Bears* and *The Great Ball Game***

## Ed Young

**The author/illustrator of *What About Me?* p. 46 of Vol. 1**

After working for a few years in advertising, Ed Young wanted to do something that would have more impact. Children's books gave him that challenge. Mr. Young begins planning his illustrations as he thinks about the story. He then researches the subject so that his illustrations will be accurate, even if he is illustrating a fantasy or a folk tale. Ed Young was born in Tienstin, China, and grew up in Shanghai and Hong Kong. The Chinese often pair words with their painting. Mr. Young agrees with that idea. "There are things that words do that pictures never can, and likewise, there are images that words can never describe." **Other books: *The Lost Horse* and *Up a Tree***

# Meet Authors of Fantasy and Animal Fantasy

## Carey Armstrong-Ellis

**The author/illustrator of *Prudy's Problem*, p. 202 of Vol. 1**

Carey Armstrong-Ellis collects snow globes and funny salt and pepper shakers. Her daughters also collect things. They inspired her to write the story *Prudy's Problem.* Ms. Armstrong-Ellis painted the pictures for her book much later. **Other books about collecting:** *Let's Go Rock Collecting* and *Collecting Baseball Cards*

## Campbell Geeslin

**The author of *Elena's Serenade*, p. 384 of Vol. 2**

Campbell Geeslin grew up in western Texas. One of Mr. Geeslin's stories, *How Nanita Learned to Make Flan,* has been made into an opera. Mr. Geeslin wrote the libretto (the words that are sung) for the opera.

**Other books:** *In Rosa's Mexico* and *On Ramón's Farm*

## Christopher Myers

**The author/illustrator of *Wings*, p. 16 of Vol. 2**

Christopher Myers is an award-winning author and illustrator. He uses cut paper, photographs, wallpaper, woodcuts, and paint to illustrate his stories. Mr. Myers's father, Walter Dean Myers, is a famous children's author. At first Christopher helped his father by doing research for him. Then he illustrated one of his father's books. Later, they worked as a team on a book. Now Mr. Myers writes and illustrates his own books. **Other books:** *Fly* and *Black Cat*

## Janet Stevens

**The author/illustrator of *Tops and Bottoms*, p. 228 of Vol. 1**

When Janet Stevens began writing *Tops and Bottoms,* the words just would not come to her, so she started by drawing the pictures. "Drawing pictures first of Bear and Hare helped me get to know them. As I dressed them up and knew their personalities, they started to talk. Then I could write the story." Ms. Stevens likes us to learn about the characters through her drawings. "When I draw characters, I like to exaggerate their personalities." You can see this in the very sleepy bear and the very energetic hare in *Tops and Bottoms.*

**Other books: *The Tortoise and the Hare* and *Coyote Steals the Blanket***

## Chris Van Allsburg

**The author/illustrator of *Two Bad Ants*, p. 358 of Vol. 2**

Chris Van Allsburg says that in grade school other kids thought it was cool that he could draw. But in junior high, he stopped drawing. Learning how to play football seemed more important. Thankfully, Mr. Van Allsburg changed his mind. In college he took some art classes. That decision changed his life. He loved his art so much that he sometimes forgot his other classes.

**Other books: *The Wreck of the Zephyr* and *Just a Dream***

# Meet Authors of Expository Nonfiction and Photo Essay

### Katacha Díaz
**The author of *Talking Walls*, p. 336 of Vol. 2**

Katacha Díaz grew up in Peru and immigrated to the United States when she was 15. Moving to a new country as a teenager was hard. "My sister Ana María and I were the only Spanish-speaking students in our new school. There was a lot of peer pressure to get rid of the accent," she says. Murals have always fascinated Ms. Díaz. She especially loves the murals by Paul and David Botello because they speak of education, immigration, and hope. These themes are a big part of her own life. **Other books about murals: *The School Mural* and *Murals: Walls That Sing***

### David Harrison
**The author of *Volcanoes*, p. 384 of Vol. 1**

David Harrison has always been interested in nature. "I began collecting bits of nature as a third grader." It started with insects. But then it grew into "just about anything I could carry home and convince my mother to let me keep in my room." Most of his writing has been for or about kids. *Volcanoes* is one of several books in Mr. Harrison's *Earthworks* series. **Other books: *Oceans* and *Caves***

## Steve Jenkins

**The author/illustrator of *Hottest, Coldest, Highest, Deepest,* p. 40 of Vol. 2**

Steve Jenkins has always liked science and art. As a child he kept spiders and lizards, and he liked to draw and paint. His father was a scientist. "We did a lot of projects together," he said. In his books, Mr. Jenkins tries to make science fun. "Kids have a natural interest in animals and things like volcanoes," he said. He wrote *Hottest, Coldest, Highest, Deepest* partly because his son was always asking him those kinds of questions. The pictures in Mr. Jenkins's books are not drawings or paintings. They are called *collages*. Collages are made by cutting different kinds of paper and pasting them in layers. **Other books: *The Top of the World* and *What Do You Do with a Tail Like This?***

## Betty Tatham

**The author of *Penguin Chick,* p. 154 of Vol. 1**

Betty Tatham says, "I write mostly about things I like, and I love animals." When she researched penguins, she read about all seventeen species of penguins. She then chose to write about emperor penguins because they were the most interesting. "I liked the fact that the dad takes care of the egg and that the mother penguin finds her mate by listening to his voice. I liked the loving relationship both parents have with their chick." **Other books: *How Animals Shed Their Skin* and *How Animals Communicate***

# Meet Authors of Narrative Nonfiction

### Susan Kuklin
**The author/photographer of *How My Family Lives in America*, p. 174 of Vol. 2**

*How My Family Lives in America* is from a series of books Susan Kuklin did to show what children are thinking and feeling. She says, "Sanu, Eric, and April took great pride in teaching me about who they are and what makes their families distinctive. It has been a joy to know them." **Other books: *Dance* and *From Head to Toe***

### Betsy and Giulio Maestro
**The author and illustrator of *The Story of the Statue of Liberty*, p. 288 of Vol. 2**

Betsy and Giulio Maestro are husband and wife. Ms. Maestro says, "We work on so many interesting books about so many different topics that we're always learning new things." Ms. Maestro feels a special connection to the Statue of Liberty. Her grandmother saw the statue for the first time as she arrived at Ellis Island from Russia in 1918. **Other books: *The New Americans* and *The Story of Money***

### David M. Schwartz
**The author of *If You Made a Million*, p. 90 of Vol. 1**

David M. Schwartz has always asked questions. Mr. Schwartz's first book, *How Much Is a Million?*, answers some big questions. For example, if one million kids all stood one on top of the other, how tall would they be? Many kids wrote him letters about the book. They said, "What we really want to know is—how much is a million dollars?" To answer them, he wrote *If You Made a Million.*

# Meet Authors of Biography

## David Adler
**The author of *America's Champion Swimmer*, p. 90 of Vol. 2**

David Adler has written almost two hundred books! "I read every newspaper and magazine story I could find about Gertrude Ederle," he says. Some newspapers said a woman could never swim the English Channel. "My parents encouraged each of my five brothers and sisters to be individuals. As a child I was known as the family artist." Paintings and drawings he did then still hang in his parents' home. Mr. Adler recently spoke with his fourth-grade teacher. She remembered the time she went to the principal. "What should I do with Adler?" she asked. "He's always dreaming." "Leave him alone," the principal said. "Maybe one day he'll become a writer." **Other books: *The Babe and I* and *A Picture Book of Harriet Beecher Stowe***

## Carol Otis Hurst
**The author of *Rocks in His Head*, p. 64 of Vol. 2**

As a child, Carol Otis Hurst went to the library almost every day. Later, Ms. Hurst became a school librarian herself. People sometimes asked her why she hadn't written a book. "I had a lot of family stories in my head. A couple of those stories began to take shape." *Rocks in His Head* was Ms. Hurst's first book. It is the true story of her father. "He collected rocks from the time he was a small boy. He kept at it throughout his life, not caring that others thought it was a waste of time." Ms. Hurst says her father loved to learn new things. "He'd be thrilled to think kids at school were reading about him." **Other books about unique people: *Snowflake Bentley* and *Beethoven Lives Upstairs***

# Meet Illustrators

## Antonio L. Castro
**The illustrator of *Jalapeño Bagels*, p. 224 of Vol. 2**

Antonio L. Castro has illustrated many children's books. He is also an artist. His art has been displayed in museums in Texas, Mexico, Spain, and Italy. Mr. Castro was born in Zacatecas, Mexico. He now lives in Juarez, Mexico. He teaches art and local history classes to children. **Another book: *Pájaro Verde/The Green Bird***

## Normand Chartier
**The illustrator of *Night Letters*, p. 334 of Vol. 1**

Normand Chartier's award-winning work often shows the animals and landscapes around his home in Brooklyn, Connecticut. *Night Letters* gave Chartier a special opportunity. He says, "I liked the challenge of showing teeny critters along with a human child." Chartier's love of nature came in handy. He wanted to create realistic-looking insects and flowers. So he spent a lot of time on his elbows and knees studying them!
**Other books: *Gullywasher Gulch* and *This Way Home***

## Steven Kellogg
**The illustrator of *If You Made a Million*, p. 90 of Vol. 1**

Steven Kellogg's books are always full of fun. "I believe in the healing power of humor," he says. Mr. Kellogg's childhood dream was to work for *National Geographic* and draw wild animals in Africa. Instead, he decided to illustrate children's books. Mr. Kellogg has now published more than one hundred books. **Other books: *Paul Bunyan* and *Sally Ann Thunder Ann Whirlwind Crockett***

## E.B. Lewis

**The illustrator of *My Rows and Piles of Coins*, p. 120 of Vol. 1**

As early as third grade, E.B. Lewis showed great artistic talent. He decided to follow in the footsteps of two uncles who were artists. For the illustrations in *My Row and Piles of Coins*, Mr. Lewis won a Coretta Scott King Honor Award. About painting in his studio, Mr. Lewis says, "I don't know what's going to happen. The music is blasting—everything from rap to classical to jazz. Paint is everywhere. It's not a bad way to make a living." **Other books: *Talkin' About Bessie* and *The New King***

## Wendell Minor

**The illustrator of *A Symphony of Whales*, p. 358 of Vol. 1**

Wendell Minor travels all over the world to research his books. When working with Jean Craighead George on *Snow Bear* and *Arctic Son,* he went to Barrow, Alaska. Barrow is near the Arctic Circle. Those experiences helped him paint the pictures for *A Symphony of Whales*. Mr. Minor loves the outdoors. He says, "What gives me satisfaction is bringing the world of nature to children." **Other books: *Fire Storm* and *Rachel: The Story of Rachel Carson***

## David Small

**The illustrator of *The Gardener*, p. 284 of Vol. 1**

David Small illustrated the book his wife wrote—*The Gardener*. He won a Caldecott Honor for his pictures in this book. Ms. Stewart and Mr. Small live in an old house along a river in Michigan.

# Glossary

## How to Use This Glossary

This glossary can help you understand and pronounce some of the words in this book. The entries in this glossary are in alphabetical order. There are guide words at the top of each page to show you the first and last words on the page. A pronunciation key is at the bottom of every other page. Remember, if you can't find the word you are looking for, ask for help or check a dictionary.

*The entry word is in dark type. It shows how the word is spelled and how the word is divided into syllables.*

*The pronunciation is in parentheses. It also shows which syllables are stressed.*

*Part-of-speech labels show the function or functions of an entry word and any listed form of that word.*

**a·dore** (ə dôr′), *VERB.* to love and admire someone very greatly: *She adores her mother.* ❑ *VERB.* **a·dores, a·dored, a·dor·ing.**

*Sometimes, irregular and other special forms will be shown to help you use the word correctly.*

*The definition and example sentence show you what the word means and how it is used.*

## Aa

**ac·com·mo·date** (ə kom′ə dāt), *VERB.* to hold; have room for: *The airplane is large enough to accommodate 120 passengers.* ❑ *VERB* **ac·com·mo·dates, ac·com·mo·dat·ed, ac·com·mo·dat·ing.**

**a·dore** (ə dôr′), *VERB.* to love and admire someone very greatly: *She adores her mother.* ❑ *VERB* **a·dores, a·dored, a·dor·ing.**

**af·ford** (ə fôrd′), *VERB.* to have the money, means, or time for: *Can we afford a new car? He cannot afford to waste time.* ❑ *VERB* **af·fords, af·ford·ed, af·ford·ing.**

**a·mount** (ə mount′), **1.** *NOUN.* the total sum: *What is the amount of the bill for the groceries?* **2.** *VERB.* to reach; add up: *The loss from the flood amounts to ten million dollars.* ❑ *VERB* **a·mounts, a·mount·ed, a·mount·ing.**

**ant·ler** (ant′lər), *NOUN.* a bony, branching growth on the head of a male deer, elk, or moose. Antlers grow in pairs and are shed once a year. ❑ *PLURAL* **ant·lers.**

**antlers**

**anx·ious·ly** (angk′shəs lē), *ADVERB.* uneasily; with fear of what might happen: *We looked anxiously at the storm clouds.*

**ar·range** (ə rānj′), *VERB.* to put things in a certain order: *She arranged the books on the library shelf.* ❑ *VERB* **ar·rang·es, ar·ranged, ar·rang·ing.**

**as·ton·ish·ment** (ə ston′ish mənt), *NOUN.* great surprise; sudden wonder; amazement: *He stared at the Grand Canyon in astonishment.*

## Bb

**bar·rel** (bar′əl), *NOUN.* a container with a round, flat top and bottom and sides that curve out slightly. Barrels are usually made of boards held together by hoops. ❑ *PLURAL* **bar·rels.**

**bay** (bā), *NOUN.* a part of a sea or lake partly surrounded by land.

**beau·ty** (byü′tē), *NOUN.* the quality that pleases both the mind and the senses in art or nature.

**beck·on** (bek′ən), *VERB.* to signal to someone by a motion of the head or hand: *She beckoned me to follow her.* ❑ *VERB* **beck·ons, beck·oned, beck·on·ing.**

| a in hat | ō in open | sh in she |
|---|---|---|
| ā in age | ȯ in all | th in thin |
| â in care | ô in order | ŦH in then |
| ä in far | oi in oil | zh in measure |
| e in let | ou in out | ə = a in about |
| ē in equal | u in cup | ə = e in taken |
| ėr in term | u̇ in put | ə = i in pencil |
| i in it | ü in rule | ə = o in lemon |
| ī in ice | ch in child | ə = u in circus |
| o in hot | ng in long | |

423

**be·neath** (bi nēth′), *PREPOSITION.* in a lower place; below; under: *The dog sat beneath the tree.*

**blade** (blād), *NOUN.* a leaf of grass.

**bliz·zard** (bliz′ərd), *NOUN.* a blinding snowstorm with very strong, cold winds. ❑ *PLURAL* **bliz·zards.**

**bloom** (blüm), *VERB.* to have flowers; open into flowers; blossom: *Many plants are blooming early this spring.* ❑ *VERB* **blooms, bloomed, bloom·ing.**

**boom¹** (büm), **1.** *NOUN.* a deep hollow sound like the roar of cannon or of big waves: *We listened to the boom of the pounding surf.* **2.** *ADJECTIVE.* having a rapid growth: *The boom town grew quickly after the gold rush.*

**boom²** (büm), *NOUN.* a long pole or beam used to extend the bottom of a sail.

**bot·tom** (bot′əm), *NOUN.* the lowest part: *These berries at the bottom of the basket are crushed.*

**bud** (bud), *VERB.* to put forth small swellings on a plant that will grow into leaves, branches, or flowers: *The tree was budding in May.* ❑ *VERB* **buds, bud·ded, bud·ding.**

bud

**bulb** (bulb), *NOUN.* a round, underground part from which certain plants grow. Onions and tulips grow from bulbs. ❑ *PLURAL* **bulbs.**

**bun·dle** (bun′dl), *NOUN.* a number of things tied or wrapped together. ❑ *PLURAL* **bun·dles.**

**bur·y** (ber′ē), *VERB.* to cover up; hide: *He dug up an ancient ruin that had been buried long ago.* ❑ *VERB* **bur·ies, bur·ied, bur·y·ing.**

**busi·ness** (biz′nis), **1.** *NOUN.* work done to earn a living; occupation: *A carpenter's business is building.* **2.** *NOUN.* buying and selling; trade: *This hardware store does a lot of business in tools.*

**bus·tle** (bus′əl), *NOUN.* a noisy or excited activity: *There was a lot of bustle as the children got ready for the party.*

## Cc

**car·pen·ter** (kär′pən tər), *NOUN.* someone whose work is building and repairing things made of wood.

**carpenter**

**car·pet·ma·ker** (kär′pit māk ər), *NOUN.* A person who makes carpets and rugs for floors: *The carpetmaker sold us a blue carpet.*

**cat·a·logue** (kat′l ȯg), *NOUN.* a list. Many companies print catalogues showing pictures and prices of the things that they have to sell. ❏ *PLURAL* **cat·a·logues.**

**cel·lar** (sel′ər), *NOUN.* an underground room or rooms, usually under a building and often used for storage.

**chan·nel** (chan′l), *NOUN.* a body of water joining two larger bodies of water: *The small channel was too narrow for the boat's passage.*

**cheat** (chēt), *VERB.* to deceive or trick someone; do business or play in a way that is not honest: *I hate to play games with someone who cheats.* ❏ *VERB* **cheats, cheat·ed, cheat·ing.**

| a in hat | ō in open | sh in she |
|---|---|---|
| ā in age | ȯ in all | th in thin |
| â in care | ô in order | ᴛʜ in then |
| ä in far | oi in oil | zh in measure |
| e in let | ou in out | ə = a in about |
| ē in equal | u in cup | ə = e in taken |
| ėr in term | ú in put | ə = i in pencil |
| i in it | ü in rule | ə = o in lemon |
| ī in ice | ch in child | ə = u in circus |
| o in hot | ng in long | |

425

**check** (chek), **1.** *VERB.* to examine something to see if it is correct, working properly, turned on, and so on: *Always check your answers.* **2.** *NOUN.* a written order directing a bank to pay money to the person named: *My parents pay most of their bills by check.* ❑ *VERB* **checks, checked, check·ing.**

**chim·ney** (chim′nē), *NOUN.* a tall, hollow column, usually made of brick, to carry away smoke from a fireplace or furnace.

**chip** (chip), *VERB.* to cut or break off a small thin piece of something: *I chipped the cup when I knocked it against the cupboard.* ❑ *VERB* **chips, chipped, chip·ping.**

**clear·ing** (klir′ing), *NOUN.* an open space of land in a forest.

**clev·er** (klev′ər), *ADJECTIVE.* bright; intelligent; having a quick mind: *She is a clever girl to have solved that math problem.*

**clut·ter** (klut′ ər), *NOUN.* many things lying around in disorder; litter: *It was hard to find the lost pen in the clutter.*

**coarse** (kôrs), *ADJECTIVE.* rough: *Burlap is a coarse cloth.*

**coin** (koin), *NOUN.* a flat, round piece of metal used as money. Pennies, dimes, and nickels are coins. ❑ *PLURAL* **coins.**

**col·lec·tion** (kə lek′shən), *NOUN.* a group of things gathered from many places and belonging together: *Our library has a large collection of books.*

**collection**

**col·lege** (kol′ij), *NOUN.* a school of higher learning, where a person can study after high school, that gives degrees or diplomas: *After I finish high school, I plan to go to college to become a teacher.*

**con·fi·dent** (kon′fə dənt), *ADJECTIVE.* firmly believing; certain; sure: *I feel confident that our team will win.*

**con·vince** (kən vins′), *VERB.* to make someone believe something: *The mistakes she made convinced me that she had not studied her lesson.* ❏ *VERB* **con·vinc·es, con·vinced, con·vinc·ing.**

**corn·stalk** (kôrn′stȯk′), *NOUN.* the main stem of a corn plant.

**crop** (krop), *NOUN.* plants grown for food: *Wheat, corn, and cotton are major crops in the United States.* ❏ *PLURAL* **crops.**

**cud·dle** (kud′l), *VERB.* to lie close and comfortably; curl up: *The two puppies cuddled together in front of the fire.* ❏ *VERB* **cud·dles, cud·dled, cud·dling.**

**cuddle**

## Dd

**dan·ger·ous·ly** (dān′jər əs lē), *ADVERB.* not safely: *The car drove dangerously close to the wall.*

**debt** (det), *NOUN.* something owed to someone else: *He paid back all his debts.*

**dew** (dü), *NOUN.* the moisture from the air that collects in small drops on cool surfaces during the night: *In the early morning, the grass is often wet with dew.*

**dew**

| a | in hat | ō | in open | sh | in she |
|---|--------|---|---------|----|--------|
| ā | in age | ȯ | in all | th | in thin |
| â | in care | ô | in order | ŦH | in then |
| ä | in far | oi | in oil | zh | in measure |
| e | in let | ou | in out | ə | = a in about |
| ē | in equal | u | in cup | ə | = e in taken |
| ėr | in term | u̇ | in put | ə | = i in pencil |
| i | in it | ü | in rule | ə | = o in lemon |
| ī | in ice | ch | in child | ə | = u in circus |
| o | in hot | ng | in long | | |

**dime** (dīm), *NOUN.* a coin of the United States and Canada equal to 10 cents. Ten dimes make one dollar. ❑ *PLURAL* **dimes.**

**down·town** (doun′toun′), *NOUN.* the main part or business part of a town or city: *Downtown can have very bad traffic.*

**doze** (dōz), *VERB.* to sleep lightly; be half asleep: *After dinner, he dozed on the couch.* ❑ *VERB* **doz·es, dozed, doz·ing.**

## Ee

**earn** (ėrn), **1.** *VERB.* to get money in return for work or service; be paid: *She earns $175 a week.* **2.** *VERB.* to get something that you deserve: *Her hard work earned her the respect of her teachers.* ❑ *VERB* **earns, earned, earn·ing.**

**earth·quake** (ėrth′kwāk′), *NOUN.* a violent shaking or shifting motion of the ground, caused by the sudden movement of rock far beneath the Earth's surface: *Earthquakes can cause great destruction.* ❑ *PLURAL* **earth·quakes.**

**eer·ie** (ir′ē), *ADJECTIVE.* causing fear because of strangeness or weirdness: *The eerie music made the movie scarier.*

**e·nor·mous** (i nôr′məs), *ADJECTIVE.* very, very large; huge: *Long ago, enormous animals lived on the Earth.*

**enormous**

**er·rand** (er′ənd), *NOUN.* a short trip that you take to do something: *She has errands to do downtown.* ❑ *PLURAL* **er·rands.**

**e·rupt** (i rupt′), *VERB.* violently to send out steam, lava, and so on: *The volcano erupted twice last year.* ❑ *VERB* **e·rupts, e·rupt·ed, e·rupt·ing.**

**ex·cit·ed·ly** (ek sī′tid lē), *ADVERB.* with strong, lively feelings: *My heart beat excitedly as I opened the old trunk.*

**ex·cite·ment** (ek sīt′mənt), *NOUN.* a condition of having strong, lively feelings about something that you like.

**ex·pen·sive** (ek spen′siv), *ADJECTIVE.* costing a lot of money; high-priced: *My uncle has an expensive car.*

# Ff

**feat** (fēt), *NOUN.* an act that shows great skill, strength, or daring.

**fetch** (fech), **1.** *VERB.* to go and get something; bring: *Please fetch my glasses for me.* **2.** *VERB.* to sell for: *Those eggs fetched a good price.* ❏ *VERB* **fetch·es, fetched, fetch·ing.**

**fine** (fīn), *VERB.* to make someone pay money as punishment for breaking a law or regulation: *The judge fined her $50.* ❏ *VERB* **fines, fined, fin·ing.**

**fire·fly** (fīr′flī′), *NOUN.* a small insect that gives off flashes of light when it flies at night; lightning bug. ❏ *PLURAL* **fire·flies.**

**fire·works** (fīr′wėrks′), *NOUN PLURAL.* firecrackers and other things that make a loud noise or go up high in the air and burst in a shower of stars and sparks.

**fireworks**

**flip·per** (flip′ər), *NOUN.* one of the broad, flat body parts used for swimming by animals such as seals and penguins. ❏ *PLURAL* **flip·pers.**

**flut·ter** (flut′ər), *VERB.* to flap the wings: *The chickens fluttered excitedly when they saw the dog.* ❏ *VERB* **flut·ters, flut·tered, flut·ter·ing.**

| | | |
|---|---|---|
| a in hat | ō in open | sh in she |
| ā in age | ȯ in all | th in thin |
| â in care | ô in order | ᴛʜ in then |
| ä in far | oi in oil | zh in measure |
| e in let | ou in out | ə = a in about |
| ē in equal | u in cup | ə = e in taken |
| ėr in term | u̇ in put | ə = i in pencil |
| i in it | ü in rule | ə = o in lemon |
| ī in ice | ch in child | ə = u in circus |
| o in hot | ng in long | |

**force** (fôrs), **1.** *NOUN.* power; strength: *The falling tree hit the ground with great force.* **2.** *VERB.* to make you act against your will: *His boss forced him to work on Saturdays.* ❑ *VERB* **for·ces, forced, for·cing.**

**fro·zen** (frō′zn), *ADJECTIVE.* hardened with cold; turned into ice: *frozen sherbet.*

## Gg

**gar·den·er** (gärd′nər), *NOUN.* someone employed to take care of a garden or lawn.

## Hh

**har·mon·i·ca** (här mon′ə kə), *NOUN.* a small musical instrument shaped like a thick candy bar, with metal reeds. It is played by breathing in and out through openings.

**harmonica**

**hatch** (hach), *VERB.* to come out of an egg: *One of the chickens hatched today.* ❑ *VERB* **hatch·es, hatched, hatch·ing.**

**hatch**

**hu·mor** (hyü′mər), *NOUN.* the ability to see or show the funny or amusing side of things: *Her sense of humor enabled her to joke about her problems.*

## Ii

**i·mag·ine** (i maj′ən), *VERB.* to make a picture or idea of something in your mind: *We can hardly imagine life without cars.* ❑ *VERB* **i·mag·ines, i·mag·ined, i·mag·in·ing.**

**in·de·scrib·a·ble** (in′di skrī′bə bəl), *ADJECTIVE.* not able to be told about in words; beyond description.

**in·for·ma·tion** (in/fər mā/shən), *NOUN.* knowledge given or received of some future event; news: *We have just received information on the astronauts' safe landing.*

**in·spi·ra·tion** (in/spə rā/shən), *NOUN.* something that has a strong effect on what you feel or do, especially something good: *Some people get inspiration from sermons, some from nature.*

**in·ter·est** (in/tər ist), **1.** *NOUN.* a feeling of wanting to know, see, do, own, or take part in something: *He has an interest in collecting stamps.* **2.** *NOUN.* the money paid for the use of someone else's money: *The interest on the loan was 7 percent a year.*

# Jj

**jab** (jab), *VERB.* to stab with something pointed: *He was jabbing his fork into the potato.* ❑ *VERB* **jabs, jabbed, jab·bing.**

# Kk

**knowl·edge** (nol/ij), *NOUN.* what you know: *Gardeners have great knowledge of flowers.*

# Ll

**lan·guage** (lan/gwij), *NOUN.* human speech, spoken or written: *Civilization would be impossible without language.* ❑ *PLURAL* **lan·guag·es.**

**laun·dry** (lȯn/drē), *NOUN.* a room or building where clothes and linens are washed and ironed.

**laundry**

| a | in hat | ō | in open | sh | in she |
|---|--------|---|---------|----|--------|
| ā | in age | ȯ | in all | th | in thin |
| â | in care | ô | in order | ŦH | in then |
| ä | in far | oi | in oil | zh | in measure |
| e | in let | ou | in out | ə | = a in about |
| ē | in equal | u | in cup | ə | = e in taken |
| ėr | in term | u̇ | in put | ə | = i in pencil |
| i | in it | ü | in rule | ə | = o in lemon |
| ī | in ice | ch | in child | ə | = u in circus |
| o | in hot | ng | in long | | |

**la·va** (lä′və), *NOUN*. the hot, melted rock flowing from a volcano.

lava

**la·zy** (lā′zē), *ADJECTIVE*. not willing to work or move fast. *He lost his job because he was lazy.*

## Mm

**mag·ma** (mag′mə), *NOUN*. hot melted rock beneath the surface of the Earth.

**man·tle** (man′tl), *NOUN*. the layer of the Earth lying beneath the crust and above the core.

**mar·ket·place** (mär′kət plās′), *NOUN*. a place where people meet to buy and sell things: *The marketplace was very crowded.*

**mel·o·dy** (mel′ə dē), *NOUN*. a pleasing or easily remembered series of musical notes; tune.

**mend·ing** (mend′ing), *NOUN*. sewing that repairs a hole or tear: *Mother sat down on the porch to do her mending.*

**mer·chant** (mėr′chənt), *NOUN*. someone who buys and sells goods for a living: *Some merchants do most of their business with foreign countries.*

**mil·lion** (mil′yən), *NOUN* or *ADJECTIVE*. one thousand thousand; 1,000,000.

**mo·tion** (mō′shən), *VERB*. to make a movement, as of the hand or head, to get someone to do something: *She motioned to us to come over to her side of the room.* ❑ *VERB* **mo·tions, mo·tioned, mo·tion·ing.**

## Nn

**nar·ra·tor** (nar′āt ər), *NOUN*. the person who tells the story or tale: *I was the narrator in the school play.*

**nec·tar** (nek′tər), *NOUN*. a sweet liquid found in many flowers. Bees gather nectar and make it into honey.

**nick•el** (nik′əl), *NOUN*. a coin in the United States and Canada worth 5 cents. ❑ *PLURAL* **nick•els.**

**note•pad** (nōt′pad′), *NOUN*. a small book of blank or lined sheets of paper in which you write notes of things that you need to learn or remember.

**nug•get** (nug′it), *NOUN*. a small, rough piece of valuable metal ore: *gold nuggets.* ❑ *PLURAL* **nug•gets.**

**nugget**

## Oo

**o•ver•head** (ō′vər hed′), *ADVERB*. over the head; on high; above: *The stars twinkled overhead.*

## Pp

**part•ner** (pärt′nər), *NOUN*. a member of a company or firm who shares the risks and profits of the business. ❑ *PLURAL* **part•ners.**

**patch** (pach), *NOUN*. a small piece of ground that is different from what surrounds it: *We have a strawberry patch in our garden.*

**peck** (pek), *VERB*. to strike with the beak: *The baby sparrow pecks at the egg.* ❑ *VERB* **pecks, pecked, peck•ing.**

**peg** (peg), *NOUN*. a pin or small bolt of wood or metal used to fasten parts together. ❑ *PLURAL* **pegs.**

**pick¹** (pik), *VERB*. to choose; select; take the one you want from a group: *I picked a blue shirt to wear with my jeans.* ❑ *VERB* **picks, picked, pick•ing.**

**pick²** (pik), *NOUN*. a tool with a heavy metal bar pointed at one or both ends, having a long wooden handle; pickax: *The miner used his pick to break up the hard rock.*

| | | |
|---|---|---|
| a in hat | ō in open | sh in she |
| ā in age | ȯ in all | th in thin |
| â in care | ô in order | ŦH in then |
| ä in far | oi in oil | zh in measure |
| e in let | ou in out | ə = a in about |
| ē in equal | u in cup | ə = e in taken |
| ėr in term | u̇ in put | ə = i in pencil |
| i in it | ü in rule | ə = o in lemon |
| ī in ice | ch in child | ə = u in circus |
| o in hot | ng in long | |

433

**plen·ty** (plen′tē), *NOUN.* a full supply; all that you need; a large enough number or amount: *You have plenty of time to catch the train.*

**poke** (pōk), *VERB.* to push with force against someone or something; jab: *He poked me in the ribs with his elbow.*
❑ *VERB* **pokes, poked, pok·ing.**

**pos·i·tive·ly** (poz′ə tiv lē), *ADVERB.* absolutely; surely; without question or doubt.

**preen** (prēn), *VERB.* to smooth or arrange the feathers with the beak.
❑ *VERB* **preens, preened, preen·ing.**

**pros·pec·tor** (pros′pek tər), *NOUN.* someone who explores or examines a region, looking for gold, oil, uranium, or other valuable resources.

**prospector**

**Qq**

**quar·ter** (kwôr′tər), **1.** *NOUN.* one of four equal parts; half of a half; one fourth: *A quarter of an hour is 15 minutes.* **2.** *NOUN.* a coin of the United States and Canada equal to 25 cents; four quarters make one dollar. ❑ *PLURAL* **quar·ters.**

**Rr**

**raft·er** (raf′tər), *NOUN.* one of the slanting timbers that hold up a roof.
❑ *PLURAL* **raft·ers.**

**re·al·ize** (rē′ə līz), *VERB.* to understand something clearly: *I realize how hard you worked.*
❑ *VERB* **re·al·iz·es, re·al·ized, re·al·iz·ing.**

**rec·og·nize** (rek′əg nīz), *VERB.* to identify: *recognizing a person from a description.* ❑ *VERB* **rec·og·niz·es, rec·og·nized, rec·og·niz·ing.**

**rich** (rich), *ADJECTIVE.* having a great deal of money, land, goods, or other property: *That movie star is a rich man.*
❑ *ADJECTIVE* **rich·er, rich·est.**

**rook·er·y** (rùk′ər ē), *NOUN.* a breeding place or colony where other birds or animals are crowded together: *a rookery of penguins.*

rookery

## Ss

**sad·ness** (sad′nis), *NOUN.* unhappiness, sorrow.

**scat·ter** (skat′ər), *VERB.* to separate and go in different directions: *The chickens scattered in fright when the truck honked at them.* ❑ *VERB* **scat·ters, scat·tered, scat·ter·ing.**

**scoff** (skȯf), *VERB.* to make fun of something to show you do not believe or respect it; mock: *We scoffed at the idea of swimming in three inches of water.* ❑ *VERB* **scoffs, scoffed, scoff·ing.**

**shin·y** (shī′nē), *ADJECTIVE.* giving off or reflecting a bright light; bright: *A new penny is shiny.*

**shiv·er** (shiv′ər), *VERB.* to shake with cold, fear, or excitement: *I shivered in the cold wind.* ❑ *VERB* **shiv·ers, shiv·ered, shiv·er·ing.**

shiver

**shock** (shok), *VERB.* to cause to feel surprise, horror, or disgust: *That child's bad manners shocked everyone.* ❑ *VERB* **shocks, shocked, shock·ing.**

**show·er** (shou′ər), *NOUN.* rain that lasts only a short time. ❑ *PLURAL* **show·ers.**

| | | |
|---|---|---|
| a in hat | ō in open | sh in she |
| ā in age | ȯ in all | th in thin |
| â in care | ô in order | ᴛʜ in then |
| ä in far | oi in oil | zh in measure |
| e in let | ou in out | ə = a in about |
| ē in equal | u in cup | ə = e in taken |
| ėr in term | ù in put | ə = i in pencil |
| i in it | ü in rule | ə = o in lemon |
| ī in ice | ch in child | ə = u in circus |
| o in hot | ng in long | |

**skil·let** (skil′it), *NOUN*. a shallow pan with a handle, used for frying; frying pan.

**slam** (slam), *VERB*. to throw or hit something with great force: *That car slammed into a truck.* ❑ *VERB* **slams, slammed, slam·ming.**

**snug·gle** (snug′əl), *VERB*. to lie closely and comfortably together; nestle; cuddle: *The kittens snuggled together in the basket.* ❑ *VERB* **snug·gles, snug·gled, snug·gling.**

snuggle

**spell¹** (spel), *VERB*. to write or say the letters of a word in order: *Some words are easy to spell.* ❑ *VERB* **spells, spelled, spel·ling.**

**spell²** (spel), *NOUN*. a period or time of anything: *There was a long spell of rainy weather in August.*

**spoil** (spoil), *VERB*. to become bad or not good to eat: *The fruit spoiled because I kept it too long.* ❑ *VERB* **spoils, spoiled, spoil·ing.**

**sprout** (sprout), *VERB*. to produce new leaves, shoots, or buds; begin to grow: *Tulips sprout in the spring.* ❑ *VERB* **sprouts, sprout·ed, sprout·ing.**

**squid** (skwid), *NOUN*. a sea animal that looks something like an octopus but having a pair of tail fins and ten arms instead of eight. It is a mollusk.

squid

**stead·y** (sted′ē), *ADJECTIVE*. firmly fixed; firm; not swaying or shaking: *This post is as steady as a rock.*

**steep** (stēp), *ADJECTIVE*. having a sharp slope; almost straight up and down: *The hill is steep.*

**strain** (strān), *VERB*. to draw tight; stretch too much: *The weight strained the rope.* ❑ *VERB* **strains, strained, strain·ing.**

**stray** (strā), *VERB*. to lose your way; wander; roam: *Our dog has strayed off somewhere.* ❑ *VERB* **strays, strayed, stray·ing.**

**stun** (stun), *VERB*. to thoroughly shock or confuse someone: *She was stunned by the news of her friend's injury.* ❑ *VERB* **stuns, stunned, stunn·ing.**

**sup·plies** (sə plīz′), *NOUN PLURAL*. the food and equipment necessary for an army exercise, camping trip, and so on.

**sur·round** (sə round′), *VERB*. to shut something in on all sides; encircle; enclose: *A high fence surrounded the field.* ❑ *VERB* **sur·rounds, sur·round·ed, sur·round·ing.**

**sur·vive** (sər vīv′), *VERB*. to continue to live or exist; remain: *These cave paintings have survived for more than 15,000 years.* ❑ *VERB* **sur·vives, sur·vived, sur·viv·ing.**

**syc·a·more** (sik′ə môr), *NOUN*. a kind of shade tree with big leaves and bark that peels off in large patches.

**sycamores**

**sym·pho·ny** (sim′fə nē), *NOUN*. a long, complicated musical composition for an orchestra.

| | | |
|---|---|---|
| a in hat | ō in open | sh in she |
| ā in age | ȯ in all | th in thin |
| â in care | ô in order | ᴛʜ in then |
| ä in far | oi in oil | zh in measure |
| e in let | ou in out | ə = a in about |
| ē in equal | u in cup | ə = e in taken |
| ėr in term | ù in put | ə = i in pencil |
| i in it | ü in rule | ə = o in lemon |
| ī in ice | ch in child | ə = u in circus |
| o in hot | ng in long | |

## Tt

**thatch** (thach), *NOUN.* made with straw, palm leaves, and so on, for a roof or covering.

**thatch**

**thou·sand** (thou′znd), *NOUN* or *ADJECTIVE.* ten hundred; 1,000.

**thread** (thred), *NOUN.* a very thin string made of strands of cotton, silk, wool, or nylon, spun and twisted together. *She sewed the sweater with cotton thread.*

**to·ken** (tō′kən), *NOUN.* a piece of metal shaped like a coin. Tokens are used on some buses and subways instead of money. ❑ *PLURAL* **to·kens.**

**trans·lu·cent** (tran slü′snt), *ADJECTIVE.* letting light through, but not easily seen through: *Frosted glass is translucent.*

**trans·mit·ter** (tran smit′ər), *NOUN.* a device that sends out sounds, or sounds and pictures, by radio waves or by electric current: *Radio stations and television stations have powerful transmitters.*

**transmitter**

**trem·ble** (trem′bəl), *VERB.* to move with a quick shaking motion: *The leaf trembles in the breeze.* ❑ *VERB* **trem·bles, trem·bled, trem·bling.**

## Uu

**un·wrap** (un rap'), *VERB.* to open: *She unwrapped the gift.* ❏ *VERB* **un·wraps, un·wrapped, un·wrap·ping.**

## Vv

**val·ue** (val'yü), **1.** *NOUN.* the real worth of something in money: *We bought the house for less than its value.* **2.** *VERB.* to think highly of something; regard highly: *Since he is an expert, his opinion is valued.* ❏ *VERB* **val·ues, val·ued, val·u·ing.**

**vol·ca·no** (vol kā'nō), *NOUN.* a cone-shaped hill or mountain built up by lava and ash around an opening in the Earth's crust. ❏ *PLURAL* **vol·ca·noes.**

**volcano**

## Ww

**wan·der·er** (wän'dər ər), *NOUN.* human being or animal that moves here and there.

**wealth** (welth), *NOUN.* riches; many valuable possessions; property: *people of wealth, the wealth of a city.*

**wob·ble** (wob'əl), *VERB.* to move unsteadily from side to side; shake; tremble: *The baby wobbled when she began to walk alone.* ❏ *VERB* **wob·bles, wob·bled, wob·bling.**

**worth** (wėrth), **1.** *ADJECTIVE.* equal in value to: *This book is worth fifteen dollars.* **2.** *NOUN.* how much a certain amount of money will buy: *He bought a dollar's worth of stamps.*

| | | |
|---|---|---|
| a in hat | ō in open | sh in she |
| ā in age | ȯ in all | th in thin |
| â in care | ô in order | ᴛʜ in then |
| ä in far | oi in oil | zh in measure |
| e in let | ou in out | ə = a in about |
| ē in equal | u in cup | ə = e in taken |
| ėr in term | ů in put | ə = i in pencil |
| i in it | ü in rule | ə = o in lemon |
| ī in ice | ch in child | ə = u in circus |
| o in hot | ng in long | |

## Unit 1

### Boom Town

| English | Spanish |
| --- | --- |
| boom | auge |
| business | negocio |
| coins | monedas |
| fetched | traído |
| laundry | lavandería |
| mending | coser |
| pick | recoger |
| skillet | sartén |
| spell | rato |

### What About Me?

| English | Spanish |
| --- | --- |
| carpenter | carpintero |
| carpetmaker | alfombrista |
| knowledge | conocimiento |
| marketplace | mercado |
| merchant | comerciante |
| plenty | mucho |
| straying | descarriando |
| thread | hilo |

### Alexander, Who Used to Be Rich Last Sunday

| English | Spanish |
| --- | --- |
| college | universidad |
| dimes | monedas de diez centavos |
| downtown | centro |
| fined | multó |
| nickels | monedas de cinco centavos |
| quarters | monedas de veinticinco centavos |
| rich | rico |

440

## If You Made a Million

| English | Spanish |
|---|---|
| amount | cantidad |
| check | cheque |
| earned | ganado |
| expensive | caros |
| interest | interés |
| million | millón |
| thousand | mil |
| value | valor |
| worth | valdrá |

## My Rows and Piles of Coins

| English | Spanish |
|---|---|
| arranged | ordené |
| bundles | paquetes |
| dangerously | peligrosamente |
| errands | recados |
| excitedly | con emoción |
| steady | estable |
| unwrapped | desenvolví |
| wobbled | me tambaleé |

# Unit 2

## Penguin Chick

| English | Spanish |
|---|---|
| cuddles | se arrima a |
| flippers | aletas |
| frozen | congelada |
| hatch | salir del cascarón |
| pecks | picotea |
| preen | atusa |
| snuggles | se acurruca |

## A Day's Work

| English | Spanish |
|---|---|
| excitement | entusiasmo |
| gardener | jardinero |
| motioned | indicó (con un gesto) |
| sadness | tristeza |
| shivered | tiritó |
| shocked | sorprendido |
| slammed | estampó |

## Prudy's Problem and How She Solved It

| English | Spanish |
|---------|---------|
| collection | colección |
| enormous | enorme |
| realize | darte cuenta |
| scattered | desparramadas |
| shiny | reluciente |
| strain | doblarse |

## Tops & Bottoms

| English | Spanish |
|---------|---------|
| bottom | parte de abajo |
| cheated | engañaste |
| clever | listo |
| crops | cosechas |
| lazy | perezoso |
| partners | socios |
| wealth | riqueza |

## William's House

| English | Spanish |
|---------|---------|
| barrels | barriles |
| cellar | sótano |
| clearing | claro |
| pegs | clavijas |
| spoil | estropearse |
| steep | empinado |

# Unit 3

## The Gardener

| English | Spanish |
|---------|---------|
| beauty | belleza |
| blooming | floreciendo |
| bulbs | bulbos |
| doze | me quedo dormido |
| humor | humor |
| recognizing | reconocer |
| showers | lluvias |
| sprouting | brotando |

## Pushing Up the Sky

| English | Spanish |
|---------|---------|
| antlers | cuernos |
| imagined | imaginar |
| languages | idiomas |
| narrator | narrador |
| overhead | por arriba |
| (holes) poked | (agujeros) hechos |

## Night Letters

| English | Spanish |
|---------|---------|
| blade | brizna |
| budding | brotando |
| dew | rocío |
| fireflies | luciérnagas |
| flutter | agito |
| notepad | libreta |
| patch | parcela |

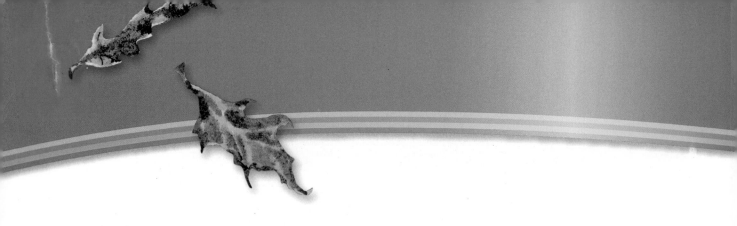

## A Symphony of Whales

| English | Spanish |
|---|---|
| anxiously | ansiosamente |
| bay | bahía |
| blizzards | ventiscas |
| channel | canal |
| chipped | picaron |
| melody | melodía |
| supplies | suministros |
| surrounded | rodeada |
| symphony | sinfonía |

## Volcanoes: Nature's Incredible Fireworks

| English | Spanish |
|---|---|
| beneath | debajo de |
| buried | enterró |
| chimney | chimenea |
| earthquakes | terremotos |
| fireworks | fuegos artificiales |
| force | fuerza |
| trembles | tiembla |
| volcanoes | volcanes |

444

# Acknowledgments

## Text

**16:** UPDATED From *Boom Town* by Sonia Levitin. Published by Orchard Books/Scholastic Inc. Copyright © 1998 by Sonia Levitin. Reprinted by permission; **38:** *The Kids' Business Book* by Arlene Erlbach. Copyright © 1998 by Arlene Erlbach. Used by permission of Lerner Publications Company, a division of Lerner Publishing Group. All rights reserved; **46:** *What About Me?* by Ed Young. Copyright © Ed Young, 2002. Published by arrangement with Philomel Books, a division of Penguin Young Readers Group, a member of Penguin Group (USA) Inc. All rights reserved; **68:** From *Alexander, Who Used to Be Rich Last Sunday.* Text copyright © 1978 by Judith Viorst. Illustrations copyright © 1978 by Ray Cruz. Reprinted with permission of Atheneum Books for Young Readers, Simon & Schuster Children's Publishing Division. All rights reserved; **90:** *If You Made a Million* by David M. Schwartz, Illustrations by Steven Kellogg, 1989. Used by permission of HarperCollins Publishers; **120:** From *My Rows and Piles of Coins* by Tololwa M. Mollel. Text copyright © 1999 by Tololwa M. Mollel. Illustrations copyright © 1999 by E. B. Lewis. Reprinted by permission of Clarion Books, a division of Houghton Mifflin Company. All rights reserved; **142:** "A Single Penny" from *The Song in My Head* by Felice Holman, 1985. Reprinted by permission of the author; **143:** "Fund-raiser" from *Almost Late to School And More School Poems* by Carol Diggory Shields, Dutton, © 2003 by Carol Diggory Shields, text. Used by permission of Dutton Children's Books, a Division of Penguin Young Readers Group, A Member of Penguin Group (USA) Inc., 345 Hudson Street, New York, NY 10014. All rights reserved. Used by permission of Ruth Cohen Inc. on behalf of the author; **144:** updated "Money" by Richard Armour from *For Partly Proud Parents: light verse about children,* with an introduction Phillis McGinley, 1950. Reprinted by permission; **145:** "coins" from *All The Small Poems and Fourteen More* by Valerie Worth. Copyright © 1987, 1994 by Valerie Worth. Reprinted by permission of Farrar, Straus & Giroux, LLC; **154:** *Penguin Chick* by Betty Tatham, illustrated by Helen K. Davie. Text copyright © 2002 Betty Tatham. Illustrations copyright © 2002 Helen Davie. Used by permission of HarperCollins Publishers; **170:** From *Seeds, Stems, and Stamens: The Ways Plants Fit into their World* by Susan E. Goodman; photographs by Michael J. Doolittle. Text copyright 2001 by Susan E. Goodman. Photographs copyright 2001 by Michael J. Doolittle. Used by permission of Millbrook Press, a division of Lerner Publishing Group. All rights reserved; **178:** *A Day's Work* by Eve Bunting, illustrated by Ronald Himler. Text copyright © 1994 by Eve Bunting. Illustrations copyright © 1994 by Ronald Himler. Reprinted by permission of Clarion Books/Houghton Mifflin Company. All rights reserved; **202:** (updated) From *Prudy's Problem and How She Solved It* by Carey Armstrong-Ellis. Published by Harry N. Abrams, Inc. Reprinted by permission; **228:** Text from *Tops And Bottoms,* copyright © 1995 by Janet Stevens, reprinted by permission of Harcourt, Inc.; **248:** "The Hare and the Tortoise" from *Aesop's Fables* selected and illustrated by Michael Hague. Specially edited text, © 1985 by Henry Holt and Company. Reprinted by permission of Henry Holt and Company, LLC.; **254:** From *William's House* by Ginger Howard, illustrated by Larry Day. Text copyright © 2001 by Ginger Howard, illustrations copyright © 2001 by Larry Day. Reprinted by permission of The Millbrook Press, Inc.; **272:** Reprinted with the permission of Atheneum Books for Young Readers, an imprint of Simon & Schuster Children's Publishing Division from *Fireflies at Midnight* by Marilyn Singer. Text copyright © 2003 Marilyn Singer; **273:** Reprinted with the permission of Atheneum Books for Young Readers, an imprint of Simon & Schuster Children's Publishing Division from *Here's What You Do When You Can't Find Your Shoe* by Andrea Perry. Text copyright © 2003 Andrea Perry; **274:** "Third-Grade Genius" from *Fearless Fernie: Hanging Out With Fernie and Me* by Gary Soto, copyright © 2002 by Gary Soto, text. Used by permission of G.P. Putnam's Sons, A Division of Penguin Young Readers Group, A Member of Penguin Group (USA) Inc., 345 Hudson Street, New York, NY 10014. All rights reserved; **284:** *The Gardener* by Sarah Stewart, pictures by David Small. Text copyright © 1997 by Sarah Stewart. Pictures copyright © 1997 by David Small. Reprinted by permission of Farrar, Straus and Giroux, LLC.; **308:** "Pushing Up the Sky," from *Pushing Up The Sky* by Joseph Bruchac, copyright © 2000 by Joseph Bruchac, text. Used by permission of Dial Books for Young Readers, A Division of Penguin Young Readers Group, A Member of Penguin Group (USA) Inc., 345 Hudson Street, New York, NY 10014. All rights reserved; **322:** Reprinted with the permission of Simon & Schuster Books for Young Readers, an imprint of Simon & Schuster Children's Publishing Division from *When The World Was Young* by Margaret Mayo, illustrated by Louise Brierley. Text copyright © 1995 Margaret Mayo. Illustrations copyright © 1995 Louise Brierley; **334:** (Updated Credit Line) From *Night Letters* by Palmyra LoMonaco, illustrations by Normand Chartier, 1996. Text © 1996 by Palmyra LoMonaco. Reprinted by permission of Palmyra LoMonaco and Normand Chartier; **352:** "dear stars" from *Dear World* by Takayo Noda, copyright © 2003 by Takayo Noda. Used by permission of Dial Books for Young Readers, A Division of Penguin Young Readers Group, A Member of Penguin Group (USA) Inc., 345 Hudson Street, New York, NY 10014. All rights reserved; **358:** Text from *A Symphony of Whales,* copyright © 1999 by Steve Schuch, reprinted by permission of Harcourt, Inc. and Steve Schuch; **376:** From "He Listens to Whales" by E. Shan Correa. Reprinted from the May 1991 issue of *Ranger Rick®* magazine, with the permission of the publisher, the National Wildlife Federation®. Copyright 1991 by the National Wildlife Federation®; **384:** Text copyright © 2002 by David L. Harrison, from *Volcanoes: Nature's Incredible Fireworks* by David L. Harrison. Published by Boyds Mill Press, Inc. Reprinted by permission; **396:** Reprinted by permission of Dr. George Pararas-Carayannis, The Tsunami Page of Dr. George PC, www.drgeorgepc.com; **396:** From "Natural Disasters," www.factmonster.com. © Pearson Education, published as Factmonster.com; **400:** "Cloud Dragons" from *Confetti Poems for Children.* Text copyright © 1996 by Pat Mora. Permission arranged with Lee & Low Books Inc., New York NY 10016; **401:** (updated) "Lemon Moon" by Beverly McLoughland, originally appeared in *Ranger Rick®,* November 1990. Reprinted by permission of the author; **402:** "springtime" from *Spin a Soft Black Song* by Nikki Giovanni. Copyright © 1971, 1985 by Nikki Giovanni. Reprinted by permission of Hill and Wang, a division of Farrar, Straus & Giroux, LLC; **403:** "Laughing Boy," original title "In the Falling Snow" by Richard Wright. Copyright © 1973 by Richard Wright. Reprinted by permission of John Hawkins & Associates, Inc.

## Illustrations

**Cover:** ©Mark Buehner; **11, 16-36** John Sandford; **62-63** Ed Parker; **65** William (Bill) Cigliano; **84-85** Jim Steck; **85** Marcel Laverdet; **117, 119** Karen Blessen; **175** Chris Van Dusen; **199-201** Stephen Kroninger; **272-274** Sachiko Yoshikawa; **279, 358-372, 444** Wendell Minor; **279, 308-320, 443** Teresa Flavin; **300-303** Jeff Mangiat; **322-328** Richard Downs; **331** Susan Swann; **378** Peter Bollinger; **388-392** Patrice Rossi Calkin.

## Photography

Every effort has been made to secure permission and provide appropriate credit for photographic material. The publisher deeply regrets any omission and pledges to correct errors called to its attention in subsequent editions.

Unless otherwise acknowledged, all photographs are the property of Scott Foresman, a division of Pearson Education.

Photo locators denoted as follows: Top (T), Center (C), Bottom (B), Left (L), Right (R), Background (Bkgd).

**4** (CL, TC, TCR) ©Ed Honowitz/Getty Images; **6** ©Jerry Lofaro/Courtesy of Konica Minolta Business Solutions, Inc./American Artists Represents; **8** ©Tim Flach/Getty Images; **10** ©Royalty-Free/Corbis; **14** ©Michael Maslan Historic Photographs/Corbis; **15** (TR) ©Michael Maslan Historic Photographs/Corbis, (T) Corbis, (BR) ©Rex L. Stevens, X-8924/Denver Public Library, Western History Collection; **38-39** Courtesy Lerner Publishing Group; **43** Getty Images; **44** Getty Images; **45** Getty Images; **66** Getty Images; **67** Getty Images; **68** Getty Images; **73-79** Getty Images; **82** Getty Images; **89** ©HIRB/Index Stock Imagery; **112** (CR, TR, TC) Getty Images; **113** (TR, BR) Kate Warren/©Museum of Mankind/British Museum/DK Images; **114** (TL) Kate Warren/©Museum of Mankind/British Museum/DK Images, (BL) Mary Evans Picture Library, (BC) Chas Howson/©The British Museum/DK Images; **115** Kate Warren/©Museum of Mankind/British Museum/DK Images; **138** Getty Images; **143** Getty Images; **144** Getty Images; **146** (BL) ©Ed Honowitz/Getty Images, (CR, BR, BC, CL, CC) Getty Images; **147** ©Ed Honowitz/Getty Images; **148** ©Jerry Lofaro/Courtesy of Konica Minolta Business Solutions, Inc./American Artists Represents; **151** (T) Digital Stock, (BR) ©Ernest Manewal/Index Stock Imagery; **152** ©Joe McDonald/Visuals Unlimited; **153** (TC) Digital Vision, (BR) ©Volvox/Index Stock Imagery; **170-173** Michael J. Doolittle Photographer; **176** ©Jules Frazier/PhotoDisc; **177** (T, TR) Getty Images, (BR) ©Rubra/Reuters/Corbis; **194** Getty Images; **195** ©CSU/Denver County Cooperative Extension Master Gardener; **196** (BL) ©Barry Runk/Stan/Grant Heilman Photography, (BC) ©Neil Hardwick/Alamy Images, (BR) ©Peggy Heard/Frank Lane Picture Agency/Corbis; **197** (CL) ©Daniel Templeton/Alamy Images, (CR) ©Alan & Linda Detrick/Holt Studios International Ltd/Alamy Images; **221** (TL) ©Linda Nicholas/ Field Museum of Natural History, (BL) Photographer John Weinstein, A113330c/Field Museum of Natural History; **222** (TR) Photographer Ron Testa, A106506c/Field Museum of Natural History, (BR) [photographer unknown], A123T/Field Museum of Natural History; **223** Photographer John Weinstein, A112444c/Field Museum of Natural History; **225** (TC, R) Getty Images, (BC) ©Amy Neunsinger/PictureArts/Corbis; **227** (TC) Getty Images, (Bkgd) Getty Images; **251** (TR, B) ©Rick D'Elia/Corbis; **252** ©Miguel Angel Munoz/Age Fotostock; **253** (TR) ©Dana Hursey/Masterfile Corporation, (BR) ©Edward Slater/Index Stock Imagery; **254** ©Comstock, Inc.; **256** ©Dana Hursey/Masterfile Corporation; **258** Getty Images; **263** Getty Images; **266** (BC) ©Comstock, Inc., (TL) Getty Images; **268** Getty Images; **270** (TL) Brand X Pictures, (TC) Getty Images, (CL) ©Idaho State Historic Preservation Office, IHSI # 85-3697; **271** (BR) Brand X Pictures, (TL) ©Marilyn "Angel" Wynn/Native Stock, (TC) North Wind Picture Archives, (TR) Corbis, (CL) ©Minnesota Historical Society/Corbis; **277** Getty Images; **278** ©Brandon D. Cole/Corbis; **279** ©Richard Ustinich/Getty Images; **281** (T, BR) Brand X Pictures; **283** (T) ©Farrell Grehan/Corbis, (BL) Getty Images; **305** (B) ©Museum of History and Industry/Library of Congress, (TCR) ©Royalty-Free/Corbis; **307** Creatas; **332** ©Royalty-Free/Corbis, **333** (CR) ©Tony Wharton/Corbis, (BCR) ©Jim Sugar/Corbis, (BR) ©Jeff Daly/Visuals Unlimited; **355** (TR) ©Art Wolfe/Getty Images, (BL) ©David B. Fleetham/Visuals Unlimited; **356** ©David Hiser/Getty Images; **357** (T) ©Maria Stenzel/NGS Image Collection, (BR) ©Kim Westerskov/Getty Images; **376** (B) ©Joe Mobley, (C) Photo obtained under N.M.F.S. permit # 987/©Flip Nicklin/Minden Pictures; **378** ©Flip Nicklin/Minden Pictures; **379** (T) ©Royalty-Free/Corbis, (TL) Photo obtained under N.M.F.S. permit # 987/©Flip Nicklin/Minden Pictures; **381** (T) Getty Images, (B) ©Danny Lehman/Corbis; **382** Corbis; **383** ©Jim Sugar/Corbis; **384** ©Richard Ustinich/Getty Images; **386** (Bkgd, BC) Getty Images; **387** ©G. Brad Lewis/Getty Images; **388** (Bkgd) Getty Images, (C) ©Matthias Kulka/Corbis; **392** ©Jonathan Blair/Corbis; **394** ©Richard A. Cooke III/Getty Images; **396** Corbis; **398** ©Juan Carlos Munoz/AGE Fotostock; **399** (CR) ©Juan Carlos Munoz/AGE Fotostock, (TR) Corbis, (CL) ©Charles O'Rear/Corbis; **404** ©Tim Flach/Getty Images; **408** ©Hans Gutknecht; **409** Houghton Mifflin Company; **411** Photo of Judith Viorst used with permission of Simon & Schuster, Inc./©Didi Cutler; **412** ©Rose Eichenbaum/Sonia Levitin; **413** ©Michael Greenlar/Courtesy, Greenfield Review Press; **420** ©Jeff Evans; **424** ©Adam Jones/Visuals Unlimited; 427 (BL) ©Kjell B. Sandved/Visuals Unlimited, (CR) ©Myrleen Ferguson Cate/PhotoEdit; **428** ©Ann Elliott Cutting/Getty Images; **429** Getty Images; **431** ©Ranald Mackechnie/Stone/ Getty Images; **432** ©E. R. Degginger/Animals Animals/Earth Scenes; **433** ©Neal Mishler/Getty Images; **434** ©David Young-Wolff/PhotoEdit; **435** Digital Vision; **436** (CL) SuperStock, (BR) ©Mike Severns/Stone/Getty Images; **437** ©Cindy Kassab/Corbis; **438** (CL) ©C. L. Smith/Visuals Unlimited, (CR) Digital Vision; **439** ©Sally Mayman; **440** Getty Images.

## Glossary

The contents of the glossary have been adapted from *Thorndike Barnhart School Dictionary,* copyright © 2001, Pearson Education, Inc.

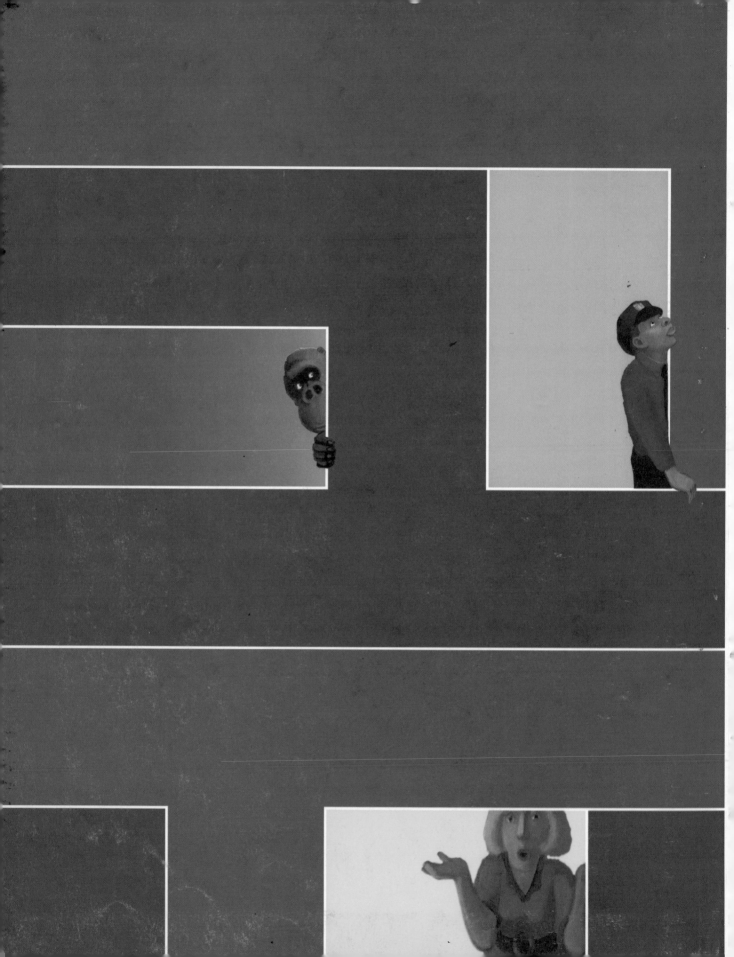